Cracking Difficult Competitors

Winning strategies to prevail over tough competitors

Tom Butler

PUSTAK MAHAL®
Delhi • Bangalore • Mumbai • Patna • Hyderabad • London

Published in India in arrangement with
Business Skills Press LLC, P.O. Box 690656, Vero Beach, Florida 32969

Publishers
Pustak Mahal®, Delhi

J-3/16, Daryaganj, New Delhi-110002
☎ 23276539, 23272783, 23272784 • *Fax:* 011-23260518
E-mail: info@pustakmahal.com • *Website:* www.pustakmahal.com

London Office
51, Severn Crescents, Slough, Berkshire, SL 38 UU, England
E-mail: pustakmahaluk@pustakmahal.com

Sales Centre
10-B, Netaji Subhash Marg, Daryaganj, New Delhi-110002
☎ 23268292, 23268293, 23279900 • *Fax:* 011-23280567
E-mail: rapidexdelhi@indiatimes.com

Branch Offices
Bangalore: ☎ 22234025
E-mail: pmblr@sancharnet.in • pustak@sancharnet.in
Mumbai: ☎ 22010941
E-mail: rapidex@bom5.vsnl.net.in
Patna: ☎ 3294193 • *Telefax:* 0612-2302719
E-mail: rapidexptn@rediffmail.com
Hyderabad: *Telefax:* 040-24737290
E-mail: pustakmahalhyd@yahoo.co.in

ISBN 978-81-223-1004-7

1st Indian Edition : January 2008

Printed at : Param Offsetters, Okhla, New Delhi-110020

Dedication

The book cover is a prism of light, photographed during the summer of 2005, on the floor of the Grand Canyon. It truly depicts the indescribable kaleidoscope of life—and the challenge of understanding the paths from which we come and where we choose to journey next.

A special thank you to the amazing people who have made this project possible: Anugito and Mary for their talent, encouragement and never ending patience; Gordon and Tony for reading countless manuscripts and sharing ideas; Hal for his wisdom and humor, he will be missed! Last but not least, we appreciate our readers and friends whose kind words speak volumes.

Table of Contents

Introduction

Competition is the engine of our economic system. Capitalism, as we know it, is powered by competition and could not exist without this struggle between opponents for economic gain. Today's global business community, which is fueled by the new communication and transportation technologies of the late 20th and early 21st centuries, is testimony to the reality of competition. Goods and services are exchanged across the globe. Go to any local merchant, supermarket or superstore and you can choose among products from every corner of the world. The exchange of products within the business-to-business environment is no different.

With competition comes a stark business reality. Some enterprises rise to meet the challenge of competition—they learn to prevail and prosper. Other organizations struggle and ultimately fail. Cruelly, yesterday's and today's victors are often tomorrow's failures. Very few business ventures have the luxury of captive or protected markets. Even those who innovate are quickly challenged by scores of individuals and companies who see success and rapidly act to share in the opportunity.

I started contemplating this book for several reasons. The bookstore shelves are replete with publications about marketing and selling (including one of mine), yet the challenge of *winning business from difficult competitors* never quite gets the discussion I believe it deserves. After all, sales and marketing success is ultimately affirmed by prevailing over your competition! I vividly recall from my time in sales that I spent extraordinary amounts of time and energy planning how I was going to beat my competition to win an order. Like most sales executives, I understood each and every order was important and precious. I certainly could have used some real help! Perhaps you can also!

The tipping point in undertaking the challenge of this book was a conversation that I had with a seventeen-year-old student on an airport shuttle bus. Having spent the day in travel hell, I finished off by finding that the last rental car was long gone, and planned to sleep for the two-hour shuttle ride home. This ball of energy was intent on telling me his life story, in which I was politely feigning interest until he began to discuss his family's local business.

"The problem with business is competition. We had two locations where we sold our merchandise. First, other merchants began to locate around our downtown store. Next, they began to copy our product line. Then, they figured out from whom we bought inventory and began selling the exact same merchandise. Finally, they undercut our prices. That was when my dad said, 'Enough!' and sold the downtown store.

He took the proceeds and bought the adjacent locations to our suburban shop so he could control the neighborhood and cut exclusive deals with our suppliers. It's no picnic, but at least we are surviving! There are just too many merchants chasing a limited number of customers!"
Sometimes we find wisdom in unexpected places from surprising people.

The competitive nature of our economy applies to local small business owners as well as the managers and owners of today's global enterprises. We will explore how to correct your competition effectively and the best ways to defend your proposals against the inevitable assaults that will be waged. Occasionally, you must walk away from a contest—we'll teach you why this strategy is important.

The central message of **Part I** is: *All competitors are not alike!* Unfortunately, we often treat them as if they are. How often have you been told to "Go beat the competition!" as if they were some monolithic entity? Chapter 1 gives you a primer on competition, the value it provides, and why it is fundamental to our economic system. Knowing the competitors, as well as you understand your own business, is the focus of Chapter 2. Knowledge can become a powerful advantage. Chapter 3 devotes significant time exploring seven basic types of adversaries, giving you an understanding of their strengths and how you can most effectively deal with each. Chapter 4 reviews the best and most difficult competitive matches.

In **Part II**, we introduce the concept that competition does not take place in a vacuum; it involves other people with distinct personalities and needs. These individuals work for or own the businesses to whom you are attempting to sell. We will examine who these business people are, what they desire and the roles they play in deciding which type of competitor will win or lose orders. I believe specific personality profiles will intuitively embrace particular competitors.

The practical challenge of winning business from the competition is the focus of **Part III**. Chapter 7 argues competing for each and every opportunity is inefficient, costly and often misguided. Chapter 8 helps you to engage your adversaries, defend your proposals, and win business without offending your prospects or customers. In Chapter 9, we explore the importance of a winning attitude and how it leverages your ability to win business.

This book is not about economic theories or suppositions. It is focused on the dynamics of competition, as it exists in an all too real business environment. It has been written for a broad business audience ranging from marketing students to executives who deal with the competition issue for each product they create, position and promote. It also applies directly to individual salesmen and saleswomen who help to create success one order at a time. The entrepreneurs and business owners who hold the ultimate stake in the success or failure of their ventures will want to know how to solve the competition puzzle.

Winning Business from Difficult Competitors is premised on the belief: *"All of your competitors are difficult and dangerous."* In fact, the only easy competitors are those who have left the business stage. Savvy business people have learned the importance of the competition challenge. They understand when to compete and how to maximize their chances of prevailing when they do. You will too!

Throughout this book I will refer to three types of people with whom businessmen and women interact. **Suspects** are people who may have a need for your product or service, but have yet to be qualified. When they are qualified, they are called **prospects.** And finally, those prospects that have decided to purchase your product are called **customers!**

BUSINESS COMPETITION

CHAPTER 1

Competition Is Fundamental And Diverse

"What I would like is to own a business that has no competitors!" How many times have you heard that statement? Or perhaps thought it yourself? What is competition? How shall we define it?

The Oxford American Thesaurus defines competition (the noun): *"competition between opponents...rivalry, vying, contest, opposition, struggle, contention, strife;* and competitive (the adjective): *a competitive industry...aggressive, dog-eat-dog, cutthroat."*

We are going to define for this text "Competitors" as those people and businesses that want to acquire your existing customers and win new potential customers. They seek to achieve economic gain through their actions. Their interests will come first and be at your expense!

You may have a single competitor or dozens of contestants. They may be local or from halfway around the globe. They may offer a similar product or a different approach to the same potential customer need. The branding, pricing or packaging may be similar or radically different. The only certainty is that they will exist!

What trends are driving competition in many markets? I believe each of these realities is impacting the competitive nature of countless business ventures:

- The shrinking global village
- Growth of entrepreneurship
- Expansion of knowledge sources and information
- Shorter product lifecycles
- Global labor and demographic shifts
- The new manufacturing model
- Customers with more choices and less loyalty
- Government policy initiatives

The shrinking global village:

A century ago, before the widespread acceptance of the airplane, automobile, telephone and electricity, most business was local. It was possible for local markets to be controlled by local enterprises. Many towns had *one* food market, *one* livery, etc. In larger cities, local neighborhood barriers protected merchants. The technologies of the 1950's began to shrink the globe. Jet airplanes, computers, efficient long-distance telephone services and the television began to open the barriers of distance and time. Local trade protection began to crumble as nation-states embraced more open trade policies. Large corporations began to expand from a national focus to broad global markets as they sought greater profits.

The wired world of the late 20th century drew even the remotest parts of the world into a global village. Personal computers, the Internet, cellular phones, and commercial satellite communications all made the normal pace of business instantaneous and real time. Goods and services were manufactured using just-in-time supply-chain economics and delivered overnight from anyplace on earth.

Today, business and consumers alike have access to countless products literally at their fingertips. Prices, delivery terms, and financing have become commodities. Whatever a consumer needs, they can find. Control of markets has to be earned rather than inherited through natural barriers to competition.

Growth of entrepreneurship:

It is no secret most new jobs are being created by small business. Global corporations have been and will continue to shrink their employment ranks. A generation of workers is migrating from seeking employment at large companies to espousing the value of being self-employed professionals or entrepreneurs. Their dream is to own or work for a small business.

They are starting new companies at record levels. A virtual army of entrepreneurs is looking for new product or service opportunities. These businesspeople are also recreating, modifying and revitalizing old business models. They intend to outwork and outsmart millions of existing firms. Some new entrants will achieve success; others will try and fail. Their efforts will create growth opportunities in some markets and overcrowd others. They will compete with each other and the established order!

Expansion of knowledge sources and information:

Thirty short years ago, most business people got their daily news from a local or regional newspaper. The evening news on television was controlled by a select group of national news broadcasts. Today, the options are almost limitless! You can start the business day by reading news from countless global reporting services, tune in to cable broadcasts or have current events streamed to your desktop. Busy traveling? No problem, the wireless world of information is all around you. In fact, the challenge of information overload has become a real and persistent issue. The bottom line, however, is simple: you can get as much information or access as many knowledge bases as you require. New products, scientific innovations, financial databases are all accessible and affordable. There is little that can be hidden or guarded from the reach of your competitors. The power of this new knowledge and information breaks down yet another set of barriers to competition!

Shorter product lifecycles:

A generation ago, getting your product to market *first* gave you time to enjoy an exclusive market. Now, the advantage of being first is much less significant. Your potential adversaries will be quicker to discover your solution and will rapidly react with a competing offering. They will emulate your success and work to improve upon it. Within months rather than years, your customers will be hard pressed to remember who came to market first. They will focus instead on price, quality, support and reputation. It's why so many successful business owners will testify time and again that constantly reinventing themselves and obsoleting their own products are at the core of their competitive strategies.

Global labor and demographic shifts:

Two trends in the labor markets have a real competitive impact. Highly skilled labor is increasingly available in the third world at costs that are a fraction of those in western employment markets. Being an established company can become a competitive disadvantage because of the structure of your labor costs. High-quality products and services are coming from markets that only a generation ago provided little beyond raw materials to western economies. These products are easily accessible in our wired world. Second, in North America, more workers are now part-time or temporary employees who do not receive access to traditional benefit programs. Many businesses are using this reality to reduce their cost structure. Sometimes the new cost structure sustains the ability to remain competitive. Businesses that have tapped into either or both of these trends have a competitive cost advantage that can be used to lower prices and dislodge adversaries.

Population demographics are constantly changing. Immigrants arrive from foreign lands, city dwellers move to the suburbs, inner city neighborhoods revitalize, and people flock to Sunbelt communities.

The baby boom generation has created societal changes since it arrived on the scene in the early 1950's. The approach of retirement for this massive population has already created enormous demands for health care services, leisure activities and housing. Each of these population flows affects competitive opportunities. Demand for new products is created while other opportunities wither.

The new manufacturing model:

Several generations ago, most manufacturing operations were clustered around geographic proximities. Transportation logistics, inventory requirements and the availability of skilled workers drove this reality. Entire states or cities were renowned for their concentration of automotive, steel, paper mills, financial and energy companies. Generations of workers spent their careers in these local factories.

The new model prescribes that manufacturing itself may be outsourced to partners or vendors who specialize in this activity–no longer a core asset every business needs to own. Facilities can be built close to transportation hubs, or supply chain partners. Locations with a plentiful supply of low-cost skilled labor or providing enterprise zones replete with generous tax and cost incentives are popular. Inventories are managed by sophisticated systems and kept to just-in-time minimal levels needed for highly automated assembly lines. The entire globe is available for the business choices, which reduce the cost of manufacturing.

Customers with more choices and less loyalty:

The challenge of keeping the customers you have has never been more acute. Why? They have a greater selection of alternatives from which to choose. Their options are not limited to just product choices, they can also choose from a selection of providers.

Tolerance for poor service or failed quality is in short supply. Consumers and business purchasers will simply not accept being ignored or being taken for granted. Acquiring new customers in this competitive environment is difficult, but it's not any easier to retain these same accounts.

In most markets, the opportunity to capture your existing customers is at the top of the competition's agenda for growth. Their marketing, promotion and advertising strategies will target these same accounts and work hard to convince them to switch! They will offer product improvements, enhancements, better service with new terms and conditions. Consumers understand this new reality and will not hesitate to change vendors. Getting a better deal, for many, has replaced the comfort of established relationships.

Government policy initiatives:

Government at the federal, state and local levels each impact the competitive landscape. How? They provide the loans, tax incentives, tariffs, regulations, and education programs to help start, finance and assist new and existing businesses. Tax policy and employment incentives are used to encourage capital spending and business growth. Legislative initiatives created The North American Free Trade Act and introduced The World Trade Organization. These controversial laws and entities have and will create enormous ongoing changes to the competitive environment. Specific markets and industries rise and fall as a result of governmental policies and intervention.

Government also purchases massive amounts of goods and services. Contracts include mandated provisions for minority-owned companies and small business owners to be a part of public works projects and many purchasing decisions. The reach of public policy initiatives is significant and it applies not just to domestic but also to international trade. Perhaps many of these initiatives benefit your company, they may also support and sustain your competitors.

Should we expect to see greater levels of competition in the foreseeable future? For most business, the answer is a resounding yes! The societal and business changes we discussed are accelerating. The global village will continue to shrink; third world nations will produce more low-cost products; more entrepreneurs will emerge; and product lifecycles will continue to shrink.

There will always be competition because it's advantageous to those who purchase goods and services. The buyer may be a business entity or an individual consumer. If your product or service is unique, purchasers will demand the creation of competition where none exists. Why? Every participant in the world economic tent—consumers, business and government—wants product innovation, lower prices, more choice and faster delivery of goods and services. In other words, they want the benefits of competition!

Many of us get uncomfortable at the thought of buying goods and services from companies who have complete or near complete market ownership. We worry about the potential for price increases, failing quality and inattentive support. In general, we tolerate utilities or regulated infrastructure providers, but we're justifiably wary of the true measure of their offerings. I suspect that our collective experiences, since the "trust buster" administration of President Theodore Roosevelt, have taught us that competition is the preferable alternative to captive markets.

What has evolved is competition that is more nimble and far reaching. The natural barriers of time, geography and product lifecycles have crumbled. To achieve business success you need to deal with all those difficult competitors and prevail. A large part of your challenge is to recognize who they are and understand that you have several distinct and diverse types of competitors, each with their own set of strengths and weaknesses.

In this realm of competition, your existing customers and new prospects will be won or lost, and your business will either succeed or fail. The people who deal with the competition for most business enterprises, no matter how large or small, are the *salespeople* and *executives* that own or manage the organization. They may devote all their time or only a portion of their effort to the selling assignment. Make no mistake, however, their competitive success will become the foundation of the business.

The ability to prevail over the competition is the ultimate test of every business skill you have acquired and all the experiences you have amassed. The marketplace may be credited for determining who succeeds or fails in any venture. But at a deeper level, the ability to compete successfully is the focal point of the market's judgment.

TEST YOUR KNOWLEDGE

1. Which of the following trends are driving competition?
- ❑ The shrinking global village
- ❑ Shorter product lifecycles
- ❑ Customers with more choice and less loyalty
- ❑ All the above.

2. Thirty years ago, most business people got their daily news from a local or regional newspaper. True/False

3. Government policy has very little effect on competition. True/False

4. Manufacturing facilities are no longer a core asset every business needs to own. True/False

5. Entrepreneurship is shrinking at a rapid pace. True/False

6. Define the term "Competitors".

....

....

....

7. There will always be competition because:
- ❑ Governments always mandate its existence.
- ❑ Population demographics create it.
- ❑ It's advantageous to those who purchase goods and services.
- ❑ None of the above.

8. Acquiring new customers in this competitive environment is difficult, but it's not any easier to retain these same accounts. True/False

9. The ability to prevail over the competition is the ultimate test of every business skill you have acquired. True/False

10. Most competitors are distinct and diverse. True/False

CHAPTER 2

Knowledge – The Start Of A Competitive Edge

Understand the competition as well as you know your own business.

The business entities and people who are your competitors deserve a thorough analysis. Why? Their mission is to acquire the same new customers you will want. In addition, they would like your current accounts to become their newest customers. Sounds pretty serious! That's exactly why it deserves your full concentration.

Creating **The Competitor's Resume** will be time consuming. The analysis should be in the form of a written document, which can be frequently referenced and revised.

COMPETITOR'S RESUME

Who specifically are the competitors?

When do you compete?

What is their business history?

Who are the principals and key employees?

Where are their locations?

What business strategy and goals are they pursuing?

How strong is their financial performance?

Who are their most important customers?

How do they service and support customers?

What type of reputation do they have with customers and suppliers?

How do they perform essential marketing and promotion activities?

How do they sell their products? What are the channels to market?

What are their products?

- Build an overview statement
- Analyze each product's strengths/weaknesses
- Pricing
- Terms and conditions
- Inventory levels
- Partners and suppliers

What specific opportunities have they won at your expense?

Why do they win business?

Which competitive profile do they fit?

The Resume is designed to acknowledge a competitive business environment and the serious consequences your challengers represent. The knowledge you will accumulate in this document is the information you will need when the competitive stakes are high!

THE COMPETITOR'S RESUME

Who specifically are the competitors?

"I can't name them, but they're out there!" Unfortunately, this response is all too common and always troublesome. It's indicative of an inwardly focused business—a firm more concerned with internal issues and disconnected from the events occurring in the external marketplace, where prospects are making crucial decisions about goods and services.

I like to remind both executives and salespeople a crucial part of their assignment is to persuade prospects to act and ultimately to choose to do business with the company they represent. How you can accomplish this task without knowing who your competitors are and why you should prevail is a mystery to me. You cannot achieve sustainable long-term success without dealing with the competition challenge!

Earlier, we defined competitors as those who *want to acquire your existing customers and win new potential customers.* They may be down the street, around the corner or across the globe.

Start by asking fundamental questions: What are the names and addresses of these businesses? Who are these entities to which you lose orders? Should your business fail, they are the ones who will benefit directly.

Some competitors are more significant and immediate than others. When you build your list of specific competitors, those you're most frequently compared with should be at the top. Learning how to triumph frequently over their proposals will produce the most dramatic impact on your success.

How many competitors should I identify? Keep the list to no more than a half-dozen entries. You can always expand the universe of competitors you're tracking and analyzing, as you grow more proficient. For most companies and sales teams, learning how to maximize your success against six competitors will have a very positive and profound impact. Should you be able to identify only one or two competitors, just be certain you have made a diligent identification effort.

When do you compete?

We are going to define two distinct forms of competition. You may choose to refine our definitions to fit your unique business model.

Core competitors are the companies who are focused on the same prospects and customers that you target. They offer similar products and sell through the same channels. You compete against them in the vast majority of opportunities you pursue. Win an order, they lose and vice-versa. Software companies each selling a single accounts payable application exclusively to the same Fortune 1000 clients are examples of core competition.

Situational competitors are companies who compete under limited and specific circumstances. They may have product lines, which partially overlap yours. Perhaps, they sell to a segment of the target prospects to which you offer solutions. Sometimes, your product competes with only part of their proposal, but your offering is eliminated when they win business. Their channels to market are often different. Situational competitors nevertheless take both prospects and customers from your business.

Examples of situational competitors include: A local drugstore chain that sells basic lawn and garden tools competes with a local garden and nursery shop. A supermarket opens a deli department to compete with a local restaurant for the lunchtime sandwich trade. Two specialty steel manufacturers with diverse product lines overlap and fiercely compete for I-beam customers, but little else. A consulting business bundles the products of various high tech vendors; their suite of products eliminates the need for your solution, despite the fact you have a more functional offering.

The good news about core competitors is they are more readily identified. Situational competitors can require a bit more work to unearth; however, don't assume these competitors are less lethal than a core adversary. In fact, depending on your specific business, situational competitors may be your toughest and most frequent opponents!

I want to caution avoiding the common mistake of identifying 'as competitors' those organizations you may wish to emulate, but that are really not impacting your sales. In other words, don't create bogus competition.

"Years ago, I was hired to fix the sales problem at a struggling small business. Several weeks into the assignment, I realized the entire organization was obsessed with competing against IBM Corporation. Yes, the very same billion dollar global business I'm sure you recognize. Countless meetings and conversations were held to discuss what IBM was doing. How should we react to whatever announcements had been made? What was their current marketing strategy? Lacking a large dose of patience, I finally exploded and reminded my colleagues that we had never lost a single dollar to IBM, nor did we have a single product that competed with them. The silence was deafening before the company president said, 'Yes, but we want to be the

next IBM!' I replied that unless we started dealing with our real competitors, people who were taking business from us each and every day, we wouldn't survive long enough to worry about competing with IBM in five or ten years!"

Focus your efforts on identifying those entities that take business from your coffers. Define the specific circumstances under which you contend with core and situational adversaries. Once you have exposed the points of competition, you are ready to move to the next phase of discovery in **The Competitor's Resume.**

What is their business history?

Understanding the past often helps one to see present reality and forecast the future. Ask the following questions:

- How long have they been in business?
- Are they growing, stagnating or shrinking?
- Has the business model changed, evolved or remained consistent?
- Have they been more, less or a constant competitor in the last 24 months?
- Any recent events such as acquisitions, new products, financial challenges or achievements that will affect the competitive landscape?
- Has the ownership or management been stable or has it changed?

I'm sure that you can quickly think of important questions that will assist in tailoring your analysis of a competitor's present and future prospects. Remember, their success or struggles will have a direct impact on the will and ability they bring to the competitive arena. This keen understanding of the opposition's circumstances will allow you to plan a successful competitive strategy.

Who are the principals and key employees?

A successful business usually has a strong management team and ownership. When you look at your competitors and see this quality you can be sure you will be challenged. Conversely, weak or ineffective management will cripple an enterprise and dramatically limit its long-term prospects.

How do I get to know my competitor's management? You can start by finding press articles, reading published biographies and generally doing some research. If your competitor is a public company, the annual report and SEC filings will provide a wealth of information. Very often introductions occur through business associations, community service projects or trade associations. Professionals such as accountants, attorneys or consultants can pave the way for introductions.

It is also very practical to pick up the telephone and introduce yourself. Don't expect your competitors to become your friends, but that shouldn't preclude having a professional relationship. You may discover that you both want to have a chance to get acquainted and size each other up!

These same sources and your fellow employees can help you become acquainted with a competitor's key employees. The group typically includes salespeople, the marketing staff, engineers and financial specialists. Take the time to learn about their backgrounds and experience levels and compare them to your teams. Do they have skills your organization lacks or vice-versa?

Your competitor's key employees may, at the right opportunity, become an excellent source of new recruits for your own business. They will often look for new employment or promotion opportunities with competitors they respect. Hiring people with specific experience in your industry or markets can be very efficient. Their knowledge of customers, prospects and the current business environment is always valuable. Hiring a competitor's key employees is a two-way street and can be a true source of conflict.

A logical source for the expansion of your business may include the acquisition of competitors. Their current managers may, in time and circumstance, fit well as part of your team. Of course, they'll have the same motivations in getting to know your business. Personally knowing your adversaries is always beneficial.

Where are their locations?

Locations can be very important for retailers or companies dependent on convenient customer locations. A quick path to success may be to find locations not yet discovered by your competition. This *"Get there first!"* strategy allows you to take ownership of the potential customers and make the competition either dislodge you or go someplace else.

You may decide to take the opposite approach, which is to locate wherever your competition is. Did you ever wonder why at some busy intersections each corner is occupied by a bank, restaurant or gas station? In many cities and towns, the entry of one 'big box' retailer means that number two is not far behind. Shopping centers beget more shopping centers.

Companies use the geographic location of distribution centers, data centers and branch locations to grow and support their business plans. Understanding the approach your competition has selected is valuable! Ultimately, you want to get the best leverage you can from your locations and those of the opposition.

What business strategy and goals are they pursuing?

It is easier to compete successfully when you understand the game plan of your adversary. Their plan may be similar to yours or dramatically different. Once you have a sense of their strategy, it's possible to either steer clear or set a determined course to engage any particular competitor on your terms.

The plan you have embraced may take your business in a direction current competitors are unwilling or unlikely to pursue. For example, a merchant who plans to close retail stores to become a catalog-focused operation may be of little concern if your company's intention is to expand its number of retail stores. A high-tech manufacturer, who intends to discontinue the product line you currently compete over, may drop off your list of competitors when they execute this event. You may, in fact, benefit from the actions both these competitors are about to take!

Are these enterprises planning to move deeper into your market space? They may be new entrants or existing competitors moving towards your strategic direction. A software company, which is introducing a new system that competes directly with your flagship product, is a new competitive entrant. An existing restaurant that's converting from a menu style of service to a buffet, just like yours, will become a serious challenger.

Some competitors will be aggressively growth oriented, others will just seek to establish a modest market position. Having excellent products may drive some contestants; others may embrace just ordinary solutions. Pricing may be an issue with certain adversaries.

The one certainty you can anticipate is competition; and that it will constantly change, just as your own business must. The quicker you can identify who the competitors are, how they are strategically evolving and what they ultimately want, the more time you'll have to react.

How strong is their financial performance?

Businesses that cannot make a profit are challenged to remain competitive and ultimately, to survive. Finding out how your adversaries are performing can be straightforward if they are publicly traded businesses required to provide detailed financial reports. These annual reports and documents are available to shareholders as well as any interested party. You can get them on the web for free or request a copy from the company investor relations department.

Privately owned firms are more difficult to get information about. However, public records and documents can provide real insights. Business incorporation documents, property tax assessments and delinquencies, tax lien records, bankruptcy filings, various legal suits, and judgments are all part of most public records. A good business advisor, accountant or attorney can guide you through the maze of what's available and show you how to obtain the records. News coverage and public gossip will provide another source of valuable information. Are they hiring new employees, or doing lay-offs? Is the plant well maintained? Do local contractors get paid on time? Do they plan to expand the business soon?

Doing serious research and pro-actively seeking information can help you gain knowledge of how your competition is faring financially. The more you can learn, the better equipped you'll be to evaluate the staying power you're facing. A competitor with strong financial backing may require a different strategy than one who is on the verge of becoming insolvent.

I overheard this conversation not very long ago at a crowded cocktail party: "*They were the worst competitive nightmare. They had a large inventory, very low prices. It was clear they couldn't possibly make money. We finally discovered the principals were quite wealthy and making money simply was not a priority! In fact, they were quite candid that they were not interested in making a dime. The business was just a way to keep busy! Once we realized this, we shifted our focus to an adjacent niche. In time, they tired of the business...and, we moved back into the market space.*"

There are several lessons to be gleaned from this conversation. Not every competitor will have the same objectives you do. Learning their objectives and the available financial resources can help you to shape your competitive strategy. In this example, the information allowed a business to survive a serious challenge. The financial condition of your key competitors is important because it directly impacts their available business resources.

Who are their most important customers?

How do I discover who my competitor's key customers are? Watch for publicly disclosed reference lists. Everybody likes to talk about his or her customers, just listen for the disclosures. They may appear in news stories, be mentioned at association gatherings, or be part of press releases and official company announcements.

Ask other people in your business community and industry groups. Sometimes you'll discover information in unexpected conversations. A neighbor once asked me who I worked for and then proceeded to volunteer, *"You must compete with the ABC Corp, they have two really big accounts but little else!"*

Prospecting will also help you to discover your competitor's important customers. The suspects you are calling will often reveal to whom they have given their business. This information can help to build a list of each competitor's customers.

Knowing your competitor's key accounts reveals who has a need for the type of solution you provide. The challenge is to convince these same people you offer a superior alternative. I always recommend opening a dialogue with your competition's customers. If you approach them professionally, you may be pleasantly surprised to discover that you will be given an opportunity to make your case. It is not unusual for business people to want backup suppliers or to rethink a relationship. Remember, they will view competition as a positive opportunity.

Calling on your opponent's customers will give you real insight into the way others view their products and company. It will tell you about the true state of their business. Do they sell to industry leaders or laggards? Are their best customers prosperous or struggling? If your adversary's key customers are about to go out of business, you want to know! Is the list of key customers growing, stagnant or shrinking? A business that has not added new key clients is in a vulnerable position.

How do they service and support customers?

In almost every market, the ability to provide outstanding service and support is crucial to ongoing success. The complexity of products, rapid changes in product offerings intersect with the customers' need to achieve value from their purchases. Customers will demand attention and satisfaction. A competitive advantage goes to those business organizations that understand and respond positively to this reality.

Take a careful look at how your competition addresses the service challenge. Is it important to them? Do they provide local service representatives and repair facilities? Have they developed a real expertise? Are they taking unique approaches? What can you learn from their methodology?

Compare their approach and results to your own offering. Then begin to evaluate your own service and support strategy. Are you satisfied with your performance? How can you improve your record? Is it important for you to offer the best service in the market? What will the cost of this strategy be? Will your customers pay for an expanded portfolio of services? Benchmark the adversary's service and support and set your competitive position.

What type of reputation do they have with customers and suppliers?

A competitor with a great reputation and a weak product offering is more dangerous than one who sells a great product but owns a poor reputation.

Learning how the marketplace views the reputation of each key adversary is the next step in our **Competitor's Resume.** Experience shows that those with strong reputations or poor records will stand out; however, many of your competitors may not have a positive or negative perception, especially if you are in a market with a lot of competitive turn over. They may simply be unknowns!

A note of caution–this task is focused on gathering information and using this knowledge as part of your overall perspective of individual competitors. It's not about using the information to attack an opponent. Those issues will be addressed in Chapter 8.

Call on your competitor's customers and ask them if they are satisfied! You will be amazed how candidly they will respond. Dissatisfied customers will often volunteer to share their experiences with everybody! They will serve as the references your competitors hoped to keep secret. Develop a list of your adversaries unhappy customers, who will honestly voice their opinions, and you create a fair and powerful competitive advantage.

You may discover in your research that a difficult competitor has a poor reputation for after-sale service. Use this knowledge to provide your customers with excellent after-sale service. Create a positive alternative! Performing just as poorly, while telling others how bad the competition is, will do nothing but waste time and effort.

The patterns and consistency of information are critically important. In truth, rarely will any business satisfy 100% of its customers. Hearing a negative comment does not make a trend or give you indisputable evidence of a competitive advantage. Jumping to conclusions or hearing only what you want to hear is a mistake. I have watched business people intent on proving an opponent has a problem embarrass themselves by refusing to let the facts get in their way.

When you watch your competitors carefully over time, you will begin to develop a universe of comments and feedback that will point to discernable trends.

How do they perform essential marketing and promotional activities?

Everyplace I go, I see my competition! The television, billboards, newspaper advertisements, radio spots...they are very visible and very aggressive marketers!

Very few successful businesses ignore the need to embrace a marketing plan. In fact, you could argue they achieved success because they understood the importance of marketing. In its purest sense, marketing is communications. The message it communicates urges its target audience to "Buy this product!" Promotions are the planned events that support the "Buy this product!" appeals. These events may take the form of product launches, introductory offers and clearance specials.

Competitors who are marketers are generally growth oriented. They correctly view marketing as key to a greater exposure to potential new customers. Their growth will come from an expansion of the marketplace or by taking opportunities from you and other participants.

In truth, many marketing plans are not successful. The message may not appeal to the target audience, it may be unclear or misinterpreted, and sometimes the target audience may prove to be non-existent. Have you read an advertisement or listened to a commercial that makes you wonder, "What is this supposed to mean? Or asked, why should I care?"

The competition may not succeed with every campaign they present. Some may completely fail in their marketing plans and retrench their business efforts. These competitors are inherently dangerous because they are trying to grow! They stand far above those who have no marketing plan, financial resources or management commitment to market their way to growth and success.

Watch the marketing efforts of your competition. It will confirm who the ambitious entrants are and help guide you in planning your own campaigns. The success or failures they experience can assist you in making better decisions about specific promotions and target audiences.

How do they sell their products? What are the channels to market?

There are two typical forms of sales channel organizations: The *direct sales* model features a channel to market that is proprietary. This method of selling is built around employees or retained contractors who have exclusive responsibility for your product or service. They may sell in your store, call on prospects at their place of business, use the telephone or sell through a catalog or over the Internet. They work for your business. The strength of this approach is the control you retain. The challenge is often the cost of creating, maintaining and expanding the channel.

The *indirect sales* model relies upon third parties, either individuals or enterprises to sell your product. These channels include manufacturer's representatives, franchisees, distributors, and wholesalers. Your product may be repackaged or embedded in another solution. The channels are not exclusive to your product and are independent entities. The channels may purchase your product directly or accept it on a consignment basis for resale. The strength is in the leverage this approach offers; you can literally have thousands of outlets. The challenge is keeping these independent parties focused on selling your solution rather than something else.

This distinction is important for several competitive reasons: Understanding how your competition sells allows you to evaluate the opportunities offered by different sales channels. If an adversary is having enormous success using the Internet or catalogue sales, you may want carefully to examine expanding into those channels. Conversely, if your adversary closes their catalog business, it should raise your interest. There may be a positive opportunity for you, or it may reinforce a decision to stay away from that particular sales avenue. You can certainly learn from someone else's success or failures!

You will develop a sense of the trends that are taking place in your market niche. If every major competitor you have is moving to an indirect sales model, you need to ask why–what do they see as the opportunity? You may decide to reject their reasoning; but, at least, consider the potential impact of their strategy.

While, you may be comfortable with your current sales model, don't forget to ask: Is it best for your customers? Is the model convenient for the current and future customers you will compete to acquire?

Does the current sales channel give you the market position and profits needed to meet future business goals? If the competition is growing faster, has better margins and enjoys larger profits, you need to consider how you will compete with these companies in the future–right now!

What are their products?

"I have no idea who my competitors are and I do not know anything about their products. We just do not discuss those topics!"

Unknown Sales Representative

I actually had a candidate for a sales position describe this position as his approach to dealing with competitors. I understand that attacking your challengers can appear to be a negative undertaking; however, I also know that you can distinguish your company and products from your competition without engaging in negative behavior, and we will show you how to do exactly that in Chapter 8.

Not being thoroughly versed on the competitor's products and company is not acceptable. I want to know the difference between solutions before I buy something, and I suspect that you do too. Being told, *"I don't know or I will not discuss"* leaves me with a very uncomfortable problem. I am confronted with deciding if the person I am speaking with is really clueless or just behaving deceitfully. Neither choice bodes well for persuading me to become a customer. You need to be both knowledgeable and comfortable discussing your competitor's products!

- **Build an overview statement**

Learn the benefits and major features of each key product the competition sells. Your adversary may have dozens of offerings or only one. Focus on the items you most often compete against and that produce sales revenue for the opposition. A dozen solutions may quickly become only one or two top sellers. Get familiar with any new products and the discontinued lines.

Become conversant without plunging into minutia. Often your prospects only want to hear the short version of why your product is superior to the competitor's offering. They want short and concise explanations.

Here's an illustration of an overview statement:

Pro-Light was first introduced in 1982. It produces about 2000 lumens of output. A licensed electrical contractor must install both a dedicated 120-volt power line connection and a supplemental low-voltage backup system.

Easy-Light was introduced two years ago. It produces 2400 lumens. You simply plug the unit into a grounded wall socket. Our technology is fresh, easy to operate and cost efficient.

- **Analyze each product's strengths/weaknesses**

Will your prospects want to explore a product as engineers would or are they content with a big picture view? Whatever the level of detailed features and functions required to sell your product, that's the equivalent level of knowledge you will also need for the competition's offering. This challenge will be different in each market. Selling expensive high technology systems requires detailed competitive expertise, while the sale of consumer electronics may require less, and greeting cards will demand very limited knowledge of a competitor's features.

If your product does require significant competitive detail, build a comparative chart, weighing your solution to the opposition's. List the key features side-by-side so anyone can quickly determine who offers which advantages. Use the sample Competitor's Comparison form we have provided, or modify it for your specific business.

YOUR PRODUCT OR SERVICE	COMPETITOR 1	COMPETITOR 2
FEATURES (A distinct part or quality)		
FUNCTIONS (Normal use or purpose)		
BENEFITS (The advantage which results in financial profit or gain)		
OPTIONS (A feature which can be chosen)		
SERVICE/SUPPORT OFFERINGS		

(See page 42 for a sample)

The analysis is only as valuable as you allow it to be.

The challenge with creating a meaningful matrix is being intellectually honest! Leaving off several key features a competitor offers may make the matrix look good, but it will do nothing for your results. Deciding that a

particular feature is meaningless because someone else has it and you don't is dishonest and counter-productive. You are trapped in this dilemma when you hear statements such as:
"If I allow the sales team to see an accurate comparison, they'll lose confidence! The truth is we don't have the best product!"

I believe that most sales professionals want to deal with reality, rather than be treated to happy talk. Disclosing reality gives you the opportunity to work with what you have and sell it successfully—despite whatever warts or faults exist. The benefit of a well-constructed analysis is to encourage putting your best foot forward and being prepared to address honestly your product deficiencies. Then, you can decide how best to enhance and position your product's marketability and serviceability as you go forward. The very nature of competition teaches us time and again that ability to sell a product is not directly correlated to its being the best in class!

- **Pricing**

The topic of pricing is by itself the subject of a complete book. We are going to keep our discussion brief and focused on the role of pricing in competition.

The price of your product may or may not be significant to your prospects when they deliberate a choice between competing products. Certain products may be so price sensitive that the best price is crucial to making a sale. I can recall a frustrated CEO remarking at a luncheon meeting, *"Pricing is never an issue for our products, the sales staff discounts whatever the price is by at least 30% anyway!"*
His complaint was valid—smart businesspeople don't leave money on the table when it is unnecessary!

It's important to understand the prices your competitors ask for their products. If the price points are significantly different from yours, you want to try to understand why and the impact of this factor. Have they discovered a way to produce the merchandise at a significantly lower cost? Are they foregoing profits to establish a brand or market? Is pricing being used as a strategy against me? If I cut prices, do my sales go up? If I raise the price, will it cost me customers?

The message I want you to grasp is that pricing is a part of the competitive nature of business. It can be used as a tool to influence the outcome of the struggle for customers. We alluded earlier to the question of having the best of class product. Many businesses have enjoyed great competitive success by taking nothing more than an average product and selling at low prices. Learn what the opposition is doing and factor this information into your own strategy.

- **Terms and conditions**

What are the business arrangements that your opponents provide to prospective customers? Terms and conditions can have a major impact on the competitive landscape because they have a real influence on the complete purchase decision. Here is a partial list of possible terms and conditions you may extend:

- Payment options and credit
- Shipping and delivery arrangements
- Transfer of title
- Product warranty
- Maintenance agreements
- Service and repair facilities
- Education and product information
- Return/exchange policy
- Upgrades and enhancements
- Customer loyalty programs and incentives

The list for your product or industry could be simpler or much more extensive.

Here's an example of the impact terms and conditions can have. Suppose your product comes with a 30-day parts-only warranty, but your competitor provides a 5-year warranty that covers their full product for both parts and labor. Do you think this warranty will persuade customers to select the competition? I can assure you it will! Even if you have a better product at an equal price, some prospects will choose the security your opponent is offering.

Any and every one of the terms and conditions in our example can move business to an adversary. In a competitive world, you want to offer every advantage you can afford to prospective customers. Do not overlook terms and conditions.

- **Inventory levels**

Do you recall the old joke that went something like this; *I can sell this to you at a really great price...unfortunately, I don't have it!* Try telling a customer you can provide the machine part to get their main production line restarted, but the delivery will take 8 to 10 weeks. Ask an anxious consumer to wait four months to have their order filled. I guarantee your competitors will thank you!

Learn as much as possible about a competitor's history with, and approach to, inventory. Why? If they have too much merchandise, you can anticipate they'll hold aggressive sales events or cut prices to get their inventory levels down. If they are always short of merchandise and require prospects to wait for deliveries, your sales strategy may emphasize the ability to fill orders quickly without any waiting.

Inventory levels are also a window into the product sales your competitors are experiencing. Holding inventory costs capital. If the shelves or warehouses are packed full, ask yourself why? Perhaps the product in question is not selling. No inventory? The competition may be selling the product like hotcakes, or they may lack the financial ability to stock the shelves.

Most business organizations will attempt to balance the inventory levels they hold. You can best judge what is appropriate in your market and products. Competitors who are heavy (or light) on merchandise should draw your scrutiny. They may be creating an opportunity for you to leverage.

- **Partners and suppliers**

I suspect you know which competitors offer the best products and which sell third-rate merchandise. You also know the best financial institutions, accountants, lawyers and important service providers to your industry and community. Watch carefully when they are retained or released by your challengers. Ask yourself why they took this action?

Learning your competition's key partners and suppliers will reveal important information beyond their ability to compete. It will also offer you insights into their on-going business strategies.

Fundamentally, success attracts success!

"After years of competing with Bob's Tool and Die, I felt that we were finally winning more and more business. They seemed to be fading as a competitor, their inventory levels decreased; they stopped undercutting my prices, the salespeople were always coming and going. The principals were less visible in our trade associations. They had new banks and accountants each year.

When they announced they were going to feature products from the Top

Company, I knew they were finished. Top makes cheap tools with very poor reputation for quality. They may be okay for an occasional user but Bob's major industrial clients would never be satisfied with that merchandise.

I expanded my sales force and immediately started calling on their key customers with great success. Today, I am reluctant even to consider Bob's Tool and Die a viable competitor. They are focused on casual tool buyers and the do-it-yourself segment."

This parable is repeated each day in thousands of industries across the globe. Smart businessmen and women are able to acquire the knowledge that's all around them and put the pieces together to achieve a competitive insight and advantage.

What specific opportunities have they won at your expense?

This question is important at two levels. It will help you track the sales you have lost. I urge you to develop a *Lost Prospect Analysis* so you can examine the reasons your prospects tell you they have chosen a competitor. That's correct—we want to hear from the accounts that chose a competitor, in their own words, why they made the decision.

Lost Prospect Analysis

Date:	Prospect Name:	Sales Rep:	Interviewed by:

Prospect
Title
Contact info:

Position in Selling Pyramid:
❑ CEO/CFO
❑ Executive Buyer
❑ CIO
❑ Recommender
❑ Evaluator

Why were we eliminated:
❑ Planned Purchase was canceled
Why?
❑ Elected to solve the "need" in a different way.
How?
❑ Selected a competitor. Who?

The Interview

Questions; did we....		Answers	Rating 1 2 3 4 5
Sales Team	• Listen to your Business Challenges?		
	• Understand your need?		
	• Present our solution?		
	• Explain our Value Proposition?		
	• Other?		
Product Solution	• Explain our F/F/B?		
	• Meet your requirements?		
	• Perform Demonstrations?		
	• Present References?		
	• Other?		
Company	• Explain our Business Mission?		
	• Introduce our Executive Management?		
	• Discuss our Cust. Support and Service ?		
	• Other?		

Share with us what you perceive as the strengths/weaknesses of our competitor and ourselves: (continue on backside)

As painful as these conversations may be, they are invaluable to understanding the perception prospects have about your offering and the value a competitor provided.

Second, this information will help you debunk myths about the competition. Sometimes, salespeople claim to lose 'all the time' to a particular competitor, but can only name one or two specific instances. You will want to explore what is really occurring? The bottom line is simple–it's bad enough to lose to adversaries; but it's intolerable to have no idea as to why you lost. In fact, it is an open invitation to sustain more defeats!

Why do they win business?

This particular question in **The Competitor's Resume** is perhaps the most important. Each of the topics we have discussed lead to this critical discussion. Start your review by asking two questions:

- What message/advantage does the competition deliver to persuade prospects to buy their product?
- How do they dismiss me as the preferred choice?

This scorecard will assist you in picking the outstanding strengths each challenger possesses as well as his or her shortcomings. Well-organized competitors will sell to their strength and position their deficiencies as unimportant. They will also 'reveal' what they perceive or decide are your points of failure as a company and solution.

How do I find out what the competition's message/advantage is and how I'm being dismissed? You ask the competitor's customers and anyone else that is exposed to the competitive process! ...Your sales team, the opponents, ex-employees, business associates, consultants, etc. They may volunteer their vital perspective, or you may have to seek them out and request their cooperation. You will be surprised how many people and businesses will take the time to share this information.

Just be sure to behave in a sincere non-judgmental fashion, which communicates, "I just want the benefit of your input, I will not attempt to judge or dispute your decision." Many companies turn to third parties to conduct market surveys to uncover this information.

Once you understand how the challengers are winning business, you can then turn to making their job as difficult as possible and increasing your chances of winning!

Which competitive profile do they fit?

Chapter 3 will introduce and explore the seven competitive profiles in great detail. As you read that chapter, think about which profile best describes each of your key challengers, and assign a profile to each.

Before we finish, I want to share a cautionary note about competitive information and analysis. The value of all the work and information you will produce is temporal. Nothing is more dangerous than outdated competitive information! No one wants to give prospects erroneous information and destroy his or her credibility, nor does anyone benefit from learning competitive information, which has been obsolete for months or years.

Your market will dictate how frequently you need to revisit and update **The Competitor's Resume.** If you're in a dynamic environment, change will dictate frequent updates. I recommended you start by creating profiles for only your key competitors so you can get comfortable with the complete scope of updating and maintaining this informative and mandatory work.

TEST YOUR KNOWLEDGE

1. The Competitor's Resume...
   - ❑ Acknowledges a competitive business environment;
   - ❑ Accumulates knowledge about key competitors;
   - ❑ Should be a written document subject to revisions;
   - ❑ All of the above.

2. Not being able to identify your competitors is a positive sign. True/False

3. What's the difference between a core and a situational competitor?

....

....

4. Why is a competitor's business history important?

....

5. Businesses that cannot make a profit...
   - ❑ Are often the best places to work;
   - ❑ Are challenged to remain competitive and survive;
   - ❑ Usually have an excess of capital;
   - ❑ Have strong management teams.

6. The more you know about a competitor's product, the better prepared you will be to compete. True/False

7. Once you understand how the challengers are winning business, you can turn to making their job as difficult as possible and increase your chances of winning! True/False

8. Don't worry about keeping track of the deals you lose, it's yesterday's news. True/False

9. Understanding why competitors win business is critically important. True/False

10. Outdated competitive information is valuable. True/False

COMPETITOR'S

Who specifically are the competitors?

....

When do you compete?

....

What is their business history?

....

Who are the principals and key employees?

....

Where are their locations?

....

What business strategy and goals are they pursuing?

....

How strong is their financial performance?

....

Who are their most important customers?

....

How do they service and support customers?

....

What type of reputation do they have with customers and suppliers?

....

How do they perform essential marketing and promotion activities?

....

RESUME

How do they sell their products? What are the channels to market?

....

What are their products?

- Build an overview statement

....

- Analyze each product's strengths/weaknesses

....

- Pricing

....

- Terms and conditions

....

- Inventory levels

....

- Partners and suppliers

....

What specific opportunities have they won at your expense?

....

Why do they win business?

....

Which competitive profile do they fit?

....

Competitor's Comparison

YOUR PRODUCT OR SERVICE A100 Widget Transporter	COMPETITOR 1 Elite Widget Mover	COMPETITOR 2 E4300 WidgetPlatform
FEATURES (A distinct part or quality) • Kevlar coated titanium ball bearings • Titanium frame and chassis	• Steel ball bearings • Steel frame	• Aluminium ball bearings • Cast iron and concrete frame
FUNCTIONS (Normal use or purpose) • Friction proof-unlimited spin cycles • Light weight and mobile	• Replace every million cycles • Stationary	• Replace monthly • Completely immobile
BENEFITS (The advantage which results in financial profit or gain) • Never needs replacement or service • Easily relocated in production line	• Replacement cost exceeds $5000 • Relocation cost exceeds $15000	• Replacement cost $2000 • Relocation impossible
OPTIONS (A feature which can be chosen) • 6" Ball Bearing • 9" Ball Bearing • 12" Ball Bearing	• 6" Ball Bearing	• None available
SERVICE/SUPPORT OFFERINGS • Unlimited life-time warranty	• 90-day parts only warranty • Monthly service contract $2000	• 30-day parts and labor warranty • Monthly service contract $1500

Lost Prospect Analysis

Date:	Prospect Name:	Sales Rep:	Interviewed by:

Prospect

Title

Contact info:

Position in Selling Pyramid:

- ❑ CEO/CFO
- ❑ Executive Buyer
- ❑ CIO
- ❑ Recommender
- ❑ Evaluator

Why were we eliminated:

- ❑ Planned Purchase was canceled
  Why?
- ❑ Elected to solve the "need" in a different way.
  How?
- ❑ Selected a competitor. Who?

The Interview

Questions; did we....		Answers	Rating 1 2 3 4 5
Sales Team	• Listen to your Business Challenges?		
	• Understand your need?		
	• Present our solution?		
	• Explain our Value Proposition?		
	• Other?		
Product Solution	• Explain our F/F/B?		
	• Meet your requirements?		
	• Perform Demonstrations?		
	• Present References?		
	• Other?		
Company	• Explain our Business Mission?		
	• Introduce our Executive Management?		
	• Discuss our Cust. Support and Service ?		
	• Other?		

Share with us what you perceive as the strengths/weaknesses of our competitor and ourselves: (continue on backside)

CHAPTER 3

Profiling Seven Competitors

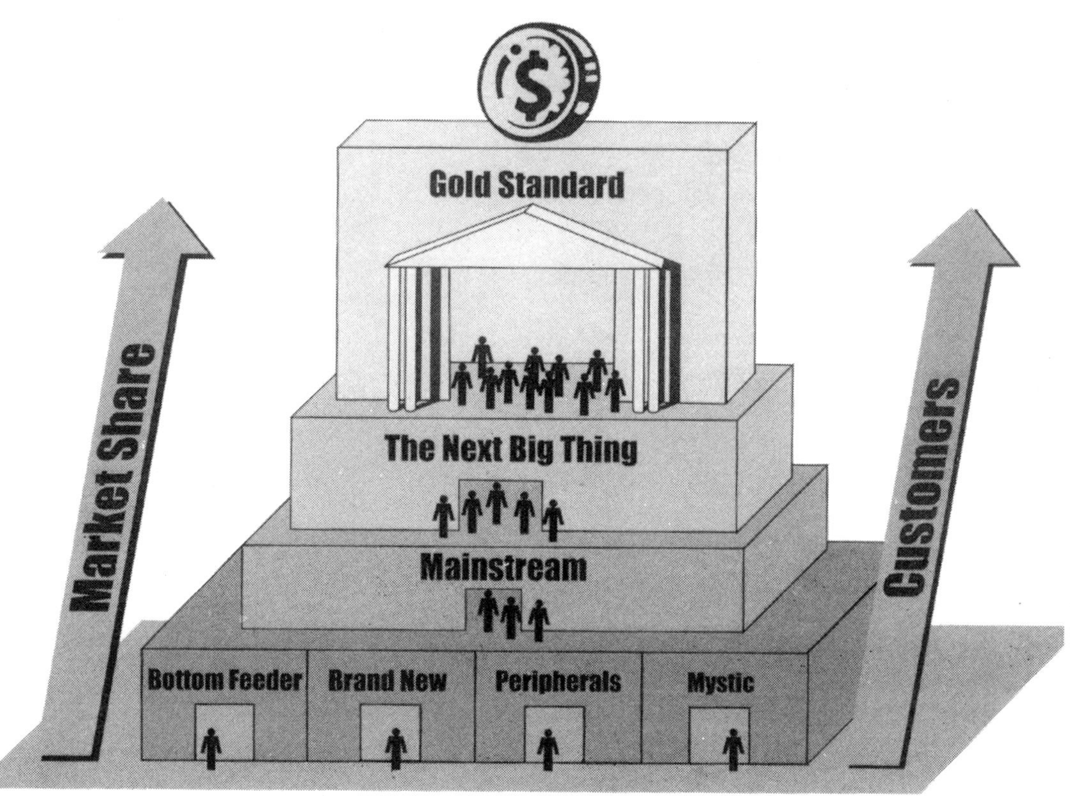

Competitors are not created equal.
They each have different needs and approaches to winning.

The stress of competition can be overwhelming. Owning a business or a sales assignment is difficult under the best of circumstances. Serious commitments of hard work, financial obligations, pride, and professional reputation are at stake. The challenge of finding prospects, qualifying, presenting your best proposal can all be rendered meaningless by four simple words: *"We chose your competitor."*

It's easy to react to the competition as if it's all one entity. It's true that all your opponents want to accomplish one result, but it is crucial to understand the different approaches they take to achieving that goal.

A quick analogy: Major League Baseball is comprised of 30 teams. They all have one goal—win games one at a time by scoring more runs than an opponent and be crowned World Champion! How they each approach winning a game is very different. Some teams feature excellent pitching, others stress defense, some may embrace a strategy of hitting home runs, while another may emphasize stealing bases and scoring one run at a time. It's exactly the same with your competitors!

The seven types of competitors:

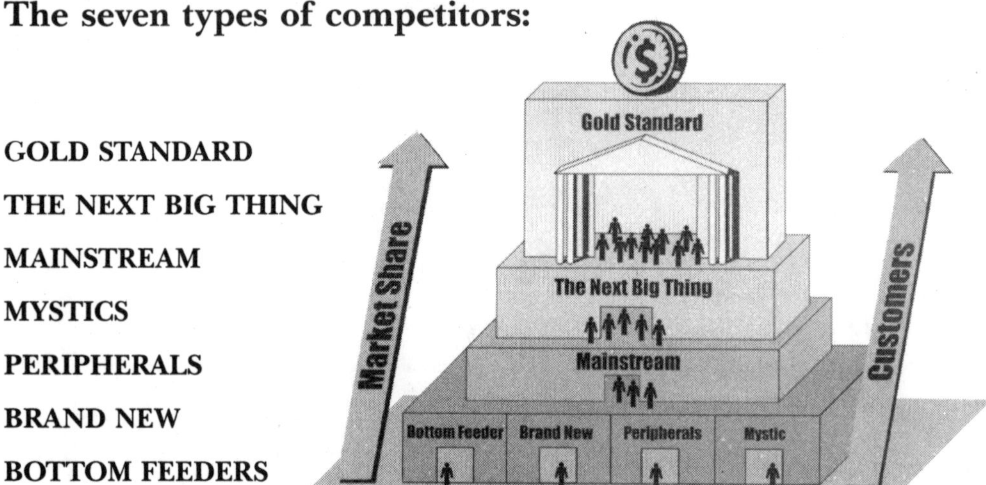

We are going to discuss each profile in detail. Our review will include clear definitions, and the exploration of what matters most to each. You will learn how to respond to challengers and what not to do. In my career, I've personally worked for and sold against each of these competitive types! I want you to learn how to maximize the opportunity to prevail against each and every adversary you encounter.

GOLD STANDARD

Definition:

Gold Standards are the owners of a market leadership position. They may be global giants that control large markets or smaller companies who establish dominance in a product niche or geographic locale. They're viewed as the safe and secure choice. *"No one ever got fired for buying from..."* or *"You can't go wrong doing business with...!"*
They enjoy name recognition and brand acceptance.

The product or service they offer may range from superior to below average. They have attained enough name recognition that they win business without offering the best solutions. The product line may be broad and diverse or quite specialized. Their competitive strategy focuses on reputation and a successful performance record.

Their success is heavily measured by profits. As the market leader, they may earn greater profits on their own than the combined results of their competitors in any given time period.

Their Goal:

The Status Quo! Life is good and above all else they want to keep the dominance they enjoy. Some Gold Standards will be very focused on growth and expansion, others will assume a more conservative and protectionist posture. Gold Standards will respond if they feel threatened by other competitors.

Competitive Strengths:

1. Well known and often respected for their achievement.
2. Viewed as thought leaders in their market segment.
3. Financial resources.
4. A reference list of customers.
5. Active marketing and promotion programs.
6. Management and employees with a depth of organizational resources at their disposal.

Competitive Weaknesses:

1. The status quo! They want to maintain both market share dominance and profit margins. It is often more difficult to sustain success than to achieve it.

2. Infrastructure works against them. To be well organized, they intentionally create organizational systems with unintended bureaucratic consequences. Ownership and management are often removed from the direct customer experience. The present employees may be very different from the team that created the original business.
3. Size often makes each customer and prospect they compete for relatively less significant and necessary.
4. The collective organizational ego begins to expect life to continue to be good! *"I did not join this company to..."* I refer to this syndrome as 'arrogance bred by entitlement'.

Their Selling Message and Competitive Positioning:

The selling message conveys safety, security and the opportunity to be part of a large customer base. The success of the business will be shared and proudly displayed. The product summary will include the subtle undertone that all these customers could not be wrong; they have chosen and are benefiting from the solution being proposed.

Should the product be questioned, prospects will be assured this is only a temporary issue and will surely be addressed. The competitors will be portrayed as representing an unnecessary degree of risk. Their strategy includes dispensing fear, uncertainty and doubts about the adversaries.

If the prospect is a current customer, the selling message will include encouragement to continue and strengthen an already successful relationship. *"The more you buy from us, the better we'll treat you!"*
The message will be sincere and reflect a real commitment.

Why They Win Business:

Gold Standards are very good at developing relationships with and selling to the top executives in their accounts. New customers choose them because they are well known, safe, predictable and beyond reproach. They may not have the best product or service, but they offer the security of a large client base and brand name recognition. The decision to purchase was too important to choose anyone else or perhaps it wasn't important enough to waste time with unknown vendors.

Current customers re-order from them or purchase additional products, because they have an existing relationship. Business as usual prevails.
"We have no reason to make a change!"

Rebutting Gold Standard:

1. Do not play by the rules set by the Gold Standard.
They want the status quo to be respected. Controlling the terms of the competition fits the internal and external environment they have in place. You do this—I do that, and my 80% market share prevails 100% of the time!

2. Turn their sales and account plans upside down.
Present your product. Offer your solution in the way that works for you and your prospect. "*Why don't I just ship you six cases of our product and let you try it out. I can stop by next week and spend a couple of hours doing some training. No obligation on your part.*" Nothing is more disruptive to the Gold Standard then having to respond to unexpected challenges. "*I am more than willing to be a secondary supplier, we'd happily accept a small order and ship on a consignment basis.*"
Be creative and resourceful. "*You can make rental payments on our equipment for 36 months and purchase for $100 at the end of the period; we don't need to be paid on delivery.*"

3. Carefully choose your battles. More than one business has been run into the ground trying to compete with the Gold Standard in situations that they cannot win. The way to break their market grip is piece-by-piece, not a broad frontal assault which plays to the strength of your opponent's resources.

Some years ago, I was invited to participate with a group of business associates in a small start-up company. The plan for the business was to get a foothold into a very big marketplace dominated by several global corporations. The product our company created was new and a significant upgrade from other competitive solutions. We had very limited financial resources, but our strategy was simple—Win one or two accounts and sell out to a global player who needed new product.

We received an inquiry from the Comptroller of a prestigious and very conservative financial institution. He asked if we could present our product immediately, he was trying to make a quick decision. The competition would be a world-class business vendor. Wanting to preserve our limited capital, I scheduled a get acquainted visit when I had other business in his vicinity. The meeting was pleasant. I asked about his needs, which were focused on specific features our product might provide. He was very clear about not wanting to make any mistakes or experience any risk, so details really mattered. His office looked like the research library of the competition—books, manuals, posters and sales souvenirs were everywhere!

"When can we get a presentation? I have to be sure everything you offer works as advertised!"

I leaned forward and said, *"Can I ask you two questions? Will you make the final decision on this purchase?"* His answer was a convincing and resounding Yes! *"Do you have the courage to purchase from a small unproven company like us, tell Mr. Global, no thanks and sustain it?"*

After a long silence and a chuckle he said, *"No, I wouldn't be comfortable with anyone but Mr. Global."*

Choose your battles.

4. Make them work hard to win the contest. Sometimes, the idea of scrapping for business is more than Gold Standard is willing to engage in. They may find it easier to concentrate on another opportunity or convince themselves the account was not all that important. Just remember the advice we discussed in #3.

5. Call on Gold Standard's customers and ask for their business.
The last thing on the agenda for most Gold Standards is defending the client base. They either want to move on to new expansionary opportunities or enjoy the current status quo. This is especially true if the current client doesn't provide a recurring sales opportunity.

When you take, or even attempt to take, customers from their portfolio, you undermine the credibility that comes with being the market leader. I can assure you every Gold Standard has clients who are unhappy and ready to switch. Take enough clients and the selling message and competitive positioning they enjoy begins to crumble!

CASE STUDY
Competing With The Gold Standard

"We, at Memory Corp., can save you significant money, our purchase price and maintenance costs are 50% lower then Mega Corporation. We aren't proposing to replace their total product line, we are asking you to give us one interchangeable piece of the production line! Incidentally, every other mill in the state has either installed, or is contracted for, our product." Tim leaned back in his chair, hung the phone up and realized Memory Corp had presented him with an opportunity.

The previous plant management had bought only the best brands of equipment. They believed revenue would grow to cover the expenses they had incurred. Unfortunately, an industry-wide glut of capacity had come online. The Canal Mill was left with a cost structure their struggling business could barely afford. Tim was recruited to fix a seriously challenged overhead structure. The board knew declining revenues and increasing costs were going to lead to losses, which were simply unsustainable.

The first series of meetings with Mega were unproductive. Tim needed cost reductions, the Mega sales team wanted new orders. Their "you need to spend to save" message had a hollow and one-sided ring. Mega had little incentive to assist his efforts; they were a market leader with an excellent reputation. The meetings had confirmed that, while they may have been sympathetic to their customer's plight, they were not going to volunteer cost reductions.

Memory Corp was a niche player with a single product that could be easily substituted into Mega's suite of production line equipment. Rob Wilson, of Memory, was a serious and seasoned sales executive. He was careful to position his offering as an enhancement to Mega delivering improved results with substantial cost reductions. His favorite sales message was "low risk and high returns." Rob was focused on prospects with a primary need to have cost reductions. Accounts with a secure financial position were often satisfied to keep their single vendor solution in place.

Mega was growing increasingly alarmed at Memory Corporation's aggressive and rapid market growth. It was clear the use of cheap 'pulp drying' units are spreading. In fact, rumors of new products targeting other segments of the production line were now circulating. A decade creating an industry-tailored and complete paper manufacturing process, and hundreds of millions of dollars of sales and profits, could be in jeopardy! Executive management wanted the momentum stopped. The Division President and VP Sales were ordered to get in front of any accounts contemplating a change and persuade the client to avoid this error. Heated discussions took place about how, specifically, to stop the momentum Memory Corp was enjoying. One thing was clear, a new low-cost product and price reductions were off the table. This was seen as a sales problem that had to be fixed with aggressive marketing and account management.

After the phone conversation that changed everything, Tim's meeting with Rob Wilson was cordial and professional. The Canal Mill needed exactly this type of opportunities. Opportunities and sales executives who could provide valuable cost savings were welcomed and esteemed. Rob knew Mega was not going to sit idly by as he courted his new prospect. He was about to change the rules of competition and that alone would set off alarm bells. His meeting with Tim and his team was coming to a close when Rob cleared his throat and announced.

"I would like to have The Canal Mill as a customer, and I understand your need to cut costs. We are willing to rent our equipment on an annual basis, with no cash upfront. We have a partner who will purchase your used Mega machines for cash within 90 days. If you want to purchase fine, but this alternative may be more attractive. I'll need an answer within 30 days." The collective gasp in the room was palpable!

Rob gave one warning before he left Tim. *" Look, you should be prepared for Mega to make this decision into a major issue. They will be extremely unhappy and very vocal about pointing out the risks they see for your business. The risks of doing business with our company are minimal and the financial rewards are significant. Mega is feeling very threatened, which they should! Please don't forget to call our references."*

The next few days were a frenzy of activity for Tim. He put together his cost justification and a transition plan for the replacement of Mega. The justification was excellent, as were Memory Corp.'s references. Rob worked tirelessly with Tim's staff, the excitement was contagious and everyone sensed a positive decision was near. Engineers and the customer support team from Memory Corp were already on site and working with their counterparts at Canal. The Mega employees were on site too, but no extraordinary efforts were apparent.

David Walker, the CEO of The Canal Mill, called Tim everyday to get an update on his progress. Today his voice was tense, *"Tim, I have some visitors from Mega in my office and I thought you may want to join us?"* Tim smiled and remembered Rob's warning.

The executives from Mega were polite but clearly on a mission. They wanted to stop the proposal and were dispensing fear and doom in generous portions. The attack on Memory Corp was relentless. The power of Mega's market dominance was on full display. A lesser business would have been hard pressed to get the audience they commanded or the leeway they were being accorded. David turned to Tim and asked very publicly, *"What do you think?"*

"I think we should leave the discussion about the risk Memory Corp presents. They have over 200 customers, including every mill in our state. What I want to know is how you gentlemen propose to save us

5 million dollars in the next 12 months? Because we cannot afford to walk away from that kind of money! David knows our alternative is to close a shift and begin the process of laying off employees. This isn't the only cost savings we need or will pursue. You have to decide whether to assist us or suffer the consequences."

Tim leaned forward and looked directly at the senior of the visitors, "*This is too important for us to play games. Either you produce a proposal to deliver $5 million, or get out of the way! We understand your message. I know you aren't happy with the decision. This isn't about Memory, Mega or anyone else...it's about our business and what we need.*"

The VP of Sales at Mega had watched this scenario play out all too often. He knew he and his salespeople were in a difficult position. Some accounts were going to choose to leave Mega because it was in their best interest. His job was to limit the damage and be as creative as possible in making an effective counter argument. *"Just remember, we build equipment that works and we support it. Our track record's impeccable! I can't save you the kind of money you are asking for and I refuse to be a poor loser, because you are and will continue to be a significant customer. I think you are being short sighted and the savings may not be without a price! I will do anything I can do to assist you should you decide to accept the Memory proposal."*

He shook Tim's hand, then David's, and the meeting ended with some pleasantries.

The Board approved the contract with Memory Corp. the next business day.

Tim called Mega to inform them of the final decision. The VP of Sales expressed his disappointment and added, *"I would like the chance to visit with you and follow your progress. If things don't work out for you, we're available on a moment's notice to help! By the way, I hope there are no hard feelings about the meeting yesterday. I have a boss and a job to perform just as you do!"*

THE NEXT BIG THING

Definition:

These players have gained market share and momentum, and are quickly achieving visibility in a competitive landscape. I sometimes refer to these competitors as 'Fashionable' or 'Trendy'.

They may be driven by a product, an innovative way of selling or a marketing message that grabs attention. I am sure you can think of countless consumer examples of the trendiest new shop, superstore, restaurant, brand of coffee, and ice cream. The business environment is replete with the same phenomena. You'll find them as local, national and global players.

The growth curve they are enjoying is unpredictable. The opportunity for market dominance exists, as does the chance for a precipitous collapse. Hot today–tomorrow passé. They may not have the profit history associated with Gold Standard; in fact, profits may be non-existent.

Their Goal:

The Next Big Thing aspires to become a market leader. The opportunity for success is so real that they will commit to an aggressive and zealous pursuit of their goal.

Competitive Strengths:

1. They have momentum and visibility, which includes favorable industry and media coverage.
2. Prospects will often view them as the trendy current choice.
3. The 'herd' mentality is a powerful sales motivator; those who miss out bear the risk of being left behind.
4. Their advocates and employees are often zealous in the commitment to achieving success–and it shows!

Competitive Weaknesses:

1. Growth and expansion is often difficult or impossible to manage effectively.
2. Time and reality will eventually expose the product limitations, quality control or service issues. Customers often have to withstand a period of retrenchment as the business and product matures.
3. Their customers may tell a different story than is being portrayed to prospects. The zeal to grow will obscure the problems being encountered by customers.
4. The financial impact of rapid growth can become a serious predicament.
5. Early products often have defects.

The Selling Message and Competitive Positioning:

The message will be one of momentum. Emphasis will be placed on the new discovery being offered and how significant the market acceptance has been. The enthusiasm will be visible and contagious.

The competitors will be portrayed as laggards that have lost touch with, or are failing to respond to, the new reality in the marketplace. Negative press reports or references, will be portrayed as unwarranted frustration, by competitors envious of success.

TNBT will speak openly about customers they have taken from competitors as a reinforcement of their momentum. Press and media accolades will be widely referenced.

Why They Win Business:

Decision makers legitimately view their offering as revolutionary. The change may transform the status quo and impact revenue, profits, operating costs or customer acquisitions. They want to enjoy some of the same momentum as TNBT.

The purchase may convey to an audience a commitment to take risk and embrace change, which is deemed important. Sometimes, being seen as trendy is personally valuable to an executive or a company.

Rebutting the TNBT:

1. **Stay on message and continue to focus on selling your value.** Momentum players thrive on being the center of competitive attention. It allows them to control the agenda of the sales process. Sell your value; let them build their own case.
2. **Find the right audience and time to *correct* TNBT message.** My advice is to wait until the prospect is ready to start the final selection process to dispel the positioning. The rebuttal must be clear, powerful and leave little time for TNBT to reposition. Deliver the rebuttal to Executive Buyers who are the decision makers.
3. **Correct the message—not the messenger or its proponents.**

   "You need to be very careful and remember..."

   - Rapid growth is a significant challenge for any business.
   - The growth may be great for TNBT, but is it beneficial for their customers? What's in this for your business?
   - The growth challenge can impact product deliveries, quality and service.
   - Have you spoken personally with their customers? (Reveal any negative references you have.)
   - What happens if this revolutionary product quickly becomes

standard fare or is by-passed by another discovery? How will this impact TNBT as a business?

- How much risk are you willing to accept?

4. **Finish the conversation with a positive discussion about your company, product, service and proposal.**

CASE STUDY
Competing With The Next Big Thing

He exclaimed boldly to the audience, *"We are growing at 30% each quarter, adding new customers each month. I ask you to consider the simple fact—all of these businesses can't be wrong! Our proposal will not get any better. Now is the time to act!"* The audience was impressed and at the same time perplexed.

Century Software was in its fifth year of existence and had emerged as a highly visible business. Their product was an innovative inventory management system. The offering was viewed as both leading edge and controversial in a marketplace that had stagnated for a decade.

Inventory Management Systems (IMS) had gained a large and comfortable leadership position since introducing the first automated system over ten years ago. The product was viewed as a standard business tool for any enterprise needing to manage large and complex inventories. The client base was a global portfolio of Fortune 5000 companies. Recently, a new version of their flagship product had been announced. It was billed as an evolutionary extension of the original system, revised to support both new platforms and business requirements.

Several executives from IMS had founded Century. They believed an opportunity existed for an innovator to offer a solution using the new wireless technology platforms now coming to market. Century had evolved from a core group of visionaries to a product driven business.

Mike Boyd had been selling for IMS for over 6 years and watching Century for the better part of 3 years. He knew in time they would come calling at his most prestigious account, New World Enterprises, a global widget manufacturer. New World had a large and diverse portfolio of products and hundreds of geographic inventory locations. Mike was anxious to get them to license his new product. He understood a smart and careful management team would insist on evaluating Century's competing solution before finalizing a decision.

"How did the Century presentation go?" Mike watched Gavin Wilcox closely.

"Are you worried, Mike?" Gavin was clearly enjoying this little chess match.

"I always worry about any competitor!" Mike and he had worked together for several years and considered each other to be professionals. They didn't always see eye-to-eye, but were mutually respective of each other's role.

"They had a lot to say some of it quite impressive. You want to make any comments?" Gavin asked.

Mike smiled broadly, *"Yeah, Gavin, a good competitor with one major problem—we're better! Let me do my presentation tomorrow, and then we can talk about as many details as you want. You may want to dress tomorrow, I'm bringing the corporate brass to the meeting."*

Mike's VP of Sales kicked off the presentation with two statements. *"First, the new product is the result of listening to our 3500 clients, including executives like Gavin Wilcox. Secondly, it's predicated on allowing you to continue your business without requiring radical operating changes, changes which could prove expensive and dangerous!"*

Mike was careful to present the key benefits of his product and reinforce the value proposition he had developed with New World's evaluation team. He had worked his audience for weeks and knew what mattered and where the areas of concern were. *"We have fixed your biggest issue with our current system!"*

"Mike, what about encrypted bar coding?"

"We're not convinced, Gavin, it's realistic or cost effective."

"Your competitor has made a big deal out of this feature."

"Well, we have a long standing policy of only selling what we can truly deliver!"

The chuckles in the room told Mike he had hit a raw nerve as intended.

Century Software was still answering questions. Stuart Green, the sales representative for Century, was growing anxious and frustrated. *"They don't seem to get the big picture, we're bogged down in details. We haven't gone through this with our other customers!"*

Mike was finishing lunch with Gavin and the Chief Financial Officer at New World. *"How do you think you're doing with your proposal?"* Mike addressed both executives, *"Look, we're long-term partners. I don't claim we're perfect, but we deliver quality programs and support them. My competitor has a different agenda–they want your business because new sales add to their cachet. We want your business because we want to continue to add value to your business and to ours. I know this application is far too important to trust to just anybody, I suspect you will ask the right questions, call your contacts and sort the hype out from reality."*

"Gavin, please don't forget—we are growing at 30% a quarter! We've already signed six new clients this month!"

The smile on Gavin's face was strained. "*Stuart, drop the 30% stuff. You have a small client base so it's easy to grow it. I need to know how many clients are in production and for how long? Here's the list of questions we need answered, in writing, by next week!"*

Stuart knew he was about to lose this deal, and he knew why. He also had one last appeal to make.

Stuart arranged for his CEO to meet with Gavin and his staff. The founder of Century Software broke the silence, *"Gavin, innovators take risk and potentially reap large rewards. It's the reason we created this unique product and are experiencing real success. Our customers are willing to make a leap of faith, even if it means we can't solve every question or demonstrate a risk-free proposal. A couple of years from now our pricing will be different. Late adopters will be presented with a perfected solution, but they'll have missed the early mover advantage! You need to trust us to deliver on our promises because it's in our and your interest to do just that. We want your business and will value your participation as a customer."*

The room was silent and the difference between a Gold Standard and Next Big Thing was laid bare.

During his evening commute Gavin weighed the risk issue. He thought about the culture at New World and how he had managed his own career. "How big a bet am I willing to make, will the potential payback be worth the risk? Can I trust Century to deliver?"

He called Mike from home and left a simple message, *"Breakfast 7:30 am at the usual place, and bring the agreement.*
Oh, congratulations!"

MAINSTREAM

Definition:

Some competitors are not interested in becoming market leaders or The Next Big Thing. Their goals are more modest and often less focused on strong growth. The business may be very profitable, well-run and offer good value to its customers. Mainstreams can often have long established histories in the marketplace and loyal customer followings.

Modest amounts of risk are acceptable. The owners/managers will not embrace strategies that will 'bet the business'. Slow and steady growth is much preferred. They can achieve prominent positions in an industry or market.

Mainstream firms, often niche to specialty product offerings, serve distinct customer profiles or geographic markets. They represent millions of enterprises in thousands of markets.

Their Goal:

Achieve profits and growth while serving their customers, prospects and employees. The long-term viability and survival of the business is paramount.

Competitive Strengths:

1. A recognized company in their market or geography.
2. A demonstrable record of product offerings, service, customers and financial sustainability. The record may range from exceptional to below average.
3. The promise of continued steady performance will appeal to an audience segment.
4. They may own well-defined marketing images and brands.

Competitive Weaknesses:

1. The demonstrable record may be inconsistent or troubled. Their reputation may also be out-of-date or inaccurate.
2. Prospects may outgrow the scope of the product or service.
   "Our needs went beyond their capacity."
3. Steady and defined may not meet the needs of every audience.
4. They may be viewed as laggards who lack the cachet of Gold Standard and The Next Big Thing.

Their Selling Message and Competitive Positioning:

Using a derivative of the Gold Standard and TNBT message, Mainstream companies will focus on the strength and safety of a known entity that's achieved marketplace recognition. Historic accomplishments and reference accounts will be stressed. The message will include the advantage of having a more personalized customer relationship and service. The selling message will also play to the risk of individual customers being overlooked by Gold Standard or poorly served by TNBT's frenzied growth.

The competitive positioning is at its most powerful when it accurately reflects a business that is focused on specific customers, products or markets.

"We will never be as large as Gold, or grow as rapidly as TNBT. We only offer unique products to a specific clientele. We are the premier choice for our target audience."

The positioning is much less powerful if it just reflects a business with a broad market and product appeal.

"We do a little bit of everything, for everybody!"

Why They Win Business:

They may be a valued part of the local business community and economy. Their relationships are often longstanding and personalized. Their most effective offer is a level of service or product specialization that's unique and important to customers.

Frequently, decision makers conclude Mainstream is, at a minimum, good enough to meet their needs. They're competitive, safe and a reasonable choice to provide a product or service.

Rebutting Mainstream:

1. **Discuss the history and track record of the business.** The performance record, accurately documented, is fair game. Mainstream will often claim to have a long business history. The claim should be explored. How many owners? How long with the current ownership group? Any bankruptcy or loan default issues?
2. **Question what the future holds for Mainstream.**
   Move the focus from past accomplishments to the challenge of the future! The resources and commitments to remain competitive in

many of today's evolving markets often require organizational resources and financial commitments far beyond those which were acceptable in the past. In your marketplace, are Mainstream competitors being consolidated?

3. **Small is not always better!** Being small does not always equate to excellent service or product innovation. Prospects may need a vendor who is a global player, or a market leader to meet their present and future business requirements.

CASE STUDY
Competing With Mainstream

Hal Ellis and his family have owned Ellis Appliances for the better part of 70 years. Hal relishes counting how many college educations, new cars and other ventures the business has funded for family, friends and employees. The store has been a fixture in Northern Arizona for longer than most building contractors can recall. This part of the West, and the store, has changed dramatically in the last ten years—larger developers and commercial projects are replacing small contractors and consumer traffic.

Kristen Ellis manages the sales function at the store. She is well known around town and aggressive when it comes to her responsibility. She also knows many out-of-town developers have minimal interest in buying locally. Sitting idly on the sidelines is not in her nature or best interest. Visiting a new timeshare site, Kristen inquired, *"Who is going to decide about the appliances for these 500 units?"*

"I really can't say, certainly it will not be me." Sheila, the sales manager, was hot and tired after a long day of escorting prospects around half-finished buildings.

"How can I find out? Look, I run a local business and it would really be an important opportunity for us. Can you make a few calls and find out?

Sheila knew it was easier to agree to help than to argue with a very determined local businesswoman.

"I will make a couple of calls this evening." She also knew Kristen would be back tomorrow and the next day, until she got her answer.

Andy Morrow was the principal interior designer for Global Time Shares (GTS); he's busy, harried and impatient on a good day. Kristen's call was not on his list of priorities. He listened to her politely.

"Thanks for asking, but we're going to use General Appliances for all of our needs. They are the manufacturer and will meet our needs just fine."

"Have they been formally awarded a bid?" Kristen inquired.

Years of experience told Andy this was not going to be as simple as he hoped.

"I don't understand why we were not included in the bidding process. We've been serving this area for 70 years with great prices and impeccable service. Our County Supervisors assured a number of local merchants we were to be included in the bidding process for any purchases of this size!"

Andy knew he had a problem and reacted quickly, *"I didn't mean to indicate the bid was let, but we always do business with General Appliances. I see no reason to change our approach, I don't have time to turn this into a big deal."*

Kristen knew she had a busy day of phone calls ahead and perhaps a few people to remind that Ellis Appliances was a substantial local employer and business community member.

When Andy's business phone rang late in the evening, it meant one thing—the boss was looking for him.

"Andy, assure me you didn't tell someone that you were too busy to entertain a local bidder for our appliances contract. Because if you did, it was a mistake that you will have to fix first thing tomorrow morning!" The line went dead and Andy knew he had a phone call to make.

Andy was his best charming self. *"Just caught me on a bad day. I'll mail you some information about the appliance specs next week!"*

Kristen was at her best and recognized a brush off.

"Andy, I'd like to drive down to meet you and spend some time talking about your appliance strategy, it'll help me make a better proposal and give us a chance to get acquainted."

The competition had been joined, as General Appliances would soon discover. General Appliances was a modestly-sized manufacturing business. They had carved a market niche out of a middle-tier product offering burdened with inconsistent quality. They always contracted service out to third party vendors. Within their industry, General was not a particularly important company. They were barely profitable and long overdue for a buyout. Industry insiders marveled that they had survived to this point.

In an earlier life, Kristen had been a research analyst on Wall Street. It only took several days to figure out who General was and what they would propose. She visited a recent GTS project and looked carefully at the appliances; candidly, they were out of place in the upscale development. She also discovered from the building supervisor that he had no service arrangement and did most repairs himself, which he was less than pleased about! Her suppliers had briefed her on General, it was clear they had a limited offering. The message she heard was simple: Get your prospect to upgrade the line and General will go away. The proposed quantities were attractive to a number of manufacturers. Ellis Appliances stocked six lines, from luxury to budget conscious. The manufacturers were anxious to get a chance to bid on this opportunity.

Hal attended every planning board meeting. The agenda revealed the CEO of GTS would be presenting this evening—an opportunity too good to pass. *"I'm Hal Ellis, I wonder if I could get ten minutes of your time? Would you actually buy 500 refrigerators, stoves, microwaves, dishwashers, etc. and have no way to service them? This isn't a big city with lots of mechanics, I know because I have done this for 70 years. In fact, I know just about every repairperson in this town because they work for me. Dust and heat—do bad things to equipment!"*

Ellen, the CEO of GTS, was about done in; a building project in a small town was not as easy as she had hoped. It was becoming downright difficult! Tonight's meeting with the planning and zoning commission was yet another example. *"Well Mr. Ellis, I guess I'll have to hire you to do just that."*

With a twinkle in his eye Hal exclaimed, *"I only service what I sell! Policy for 70 years and I don't see any good reason to change!"*

The CEO smiled and realized this was but another challenge to be faced and Andy's mistake was not about to go away.

The sales department at General Appliance was always in turmoil. Accounts were frequently turned over and managed on a transactional basis. The staff knew that each proposal was driven by the current financial condition of their employer. Sometimes they were very price sensitive, and on other occasions they were not. They liked deals that had slipped under the radar of their competition or were driven by purchasers with little time to spend on the niceties of evaluations and proposals. Get in quick, close the sale and move on was the order of the day. When Andy Morrow called to ask for a formal bid, the first question asked was why?

"We are committed to opening the process to competitive bidding," explained Andy. *"I expect that several other manufacturers will offer proposals under a general contractor bid from a local merchant."* The silence was deafening.

Ellen attended Kristen's second meeting with Andy. The atmosphere was cordial and relaxed while Kristen briefed him.

"I am prepared to propose six alternatives, with each manufacturer presenting their appropriate line. If you'd like, I can eliminate the budget or high-end lines from consideration. The manufacturers will provide extended warranties, installation and delivery support before turning maintenance and on-going service over to our team."

Ellen inquired about the pricing per unit.

"I can give each manufacturer's pricing; several of them have offered low-cost financing and deferred payment terms. My job is to give you the option to choose which alternative works best for your business. Our profit is a 15% uplift over the manufacturer's bid, straightforward with no hidden mark ups."

Andy knew Ellen well enough to notice she was impressed, and he also knew she did business with people who impressed her.

General Appliance faxed its bid in to Andy; it was brief and to the point. They refused to offer any financing, payment terms or service arrangements. *"This is our best and final offer!"* Andy wanted a presentation and face-to-face meeting, but agreeing on a scheduled time seemed impossible. An appetite for competition didn't seem to exist.

Andy received his late night phone call. Ellen had selected the high-end line Kristen proposed.

"The finance people tell me the deferred payment terms and low cost financing allow us to upgrade at no cost. Time to get the contract finished...besides, we could use some good local publicity and help from Mr. Ellis!"

MYSTICS

The Definition:

Mystics are competitors who promise a revolutionary new product or service. The offering is often viewed as a quantum leap forward and capable of changing the way business as usual is conducted. The product may represent a radically different approach to an established need; or it may be a completely new solution to a previously unmet or undiscovered need. The leaders of these businesses have a vision that foresees a departure from the current status quo.

Industries such as high technology and health care are replete with this form of competitor, but you will find Mystics across the economic spectrum. Many of the products and services we view as traditional and normal parts of everyday life are the result of yesterday's Mystics. The electric light, telephone, automobiles, airplanes, computers and countless consumer electronics are the legacy of 20th Century innovators. The Gold Standard, The Next Big Thing and Mainstream competitors of tomorrow will compete in marketplaces Mystics usher into existence. Every so often, Mystics will grow into owning the markets they create.

Their Goal:

Create unique products and services that spawn new markets. These innovations affect the way commerce is conducted and the quality of life for countless people.

Competitive Strengths:

1. The vision to see a future opportunity and marketplace.
2. The skill to translate a vision into a product or service.
3. A passion and commitment to the products they offer.
4. They often attract management and employees with very specific product skills and strong intellects.
5. The product often has a clean reference record because it's not yet released or in production.

Competitive Weaknesses:

1. The product reality often fails to meet its visionary objectives.
2. Creating and operating a successful business model can be problematic.
3. The vision may be flawed, wrong or by-passed by other products.

Their Selling Message and Competitive Positioning:

Mystics present an evangelical message with a strong appeal to those who will accept the risk of changing the status quo in their company and marketplace. The competitive appeal will remind prospects while other choices may appear safe, they're most dangerous because they offer nothing more than the status quo. Those who select the Mystic solution will be positioned to enjoy the early adoption advantages of new market leaders. "*The first organizations to offer this new benefit to their customers will gain...*"

Why They Win Business:

Decision makers are willing to embrace risk, in return for the promise of extraordinary rewards. Business people will often commit capital and effort to change agents in order to achieve a competitive advantage. The attraction of being first to gain from a new product or service is real and appealing.

Visionaries who can present a concept with tangible benefits are powerful competitors. Decision makers are often willing, and resigned, to accepting only a portion of the proposed benefits.

Rebutting Mystics:

1. **The prospect's key decision makers need to understand:**
   - The product reality will not often equate to the vision. It may take years of diligent work to get it right. Early adaptors bear the full weight of this risk.
   - Mystics may be challenged to make the transition to a customer service and support centric organization.
2. **Offer the prospect the opportunity to use your solution as a transition to Mystic.** *"You may want the benefits we can deliver now! Work with our competitor to bring their product to completion and moderate your risk."*
3. **If Mystic wins the order, leave the door open!** The prospect should feel comfortable they can re-engage with your company.

CASE STUDY
Competing With Mystics

Lloyd's sales manager was busy on the phone when he entered the office. He ignored Lloyd for the length of the conversation. Slowly he turned a cold stare at the now uncomfortable sales rep. He then broke out in a laugh and continued to laugh!

"So you're the young man who lost a deal to a company with no product and no customers! Welcome to sales! Tell me this tale from the beginning...I want to savor every detail."

Lloyd felt he had been spared, at least for now.

"It started with a phone call I got exactly a month ago from Zeb Miller at Howard Brothers. He's been a customer for years and I recently sold him a new HVAC system for the Atlanta office. He was asking about a system for a new 'green building' they were breaking ground on in Vermont. So, I sent him material on our new S6000 HVAC product.

I called him the next week and he asked a couple of questions but didn't seem ready to have me visit. Two weeks ago, I called again and offered to bring Bill Adams with me to discuss the S6000. When we finally had our meeting, Zeb started by saying this new building is leading edge and they really want break-through equipment. He asked Bill what he knew about 'UV Fluxtron' cooling and evaporation. Bill had read several articles in a scientific journal but said it was to the best of his knowledge not available in any commercial products.

Zeb started raving about a company called Crystal Power Inventions that claims to have patented a UV Fluxtron unit for green buildings. We sat there and listened to him credit this company with no less than saving the world from its next energy crisis. Every time I mentioned the S6000, he said, 'Nice product, but just more of the same technology.'

I had our research group check out this Crystal Power Inventions—No customers! Seems they have presented papers at several industry conferences and are well-respected visionaries. The top executives are all scientists and PhDs.

I visited Zeb last week and told him he was making a big mistake. The S6000 will reduce his energy consumption by 20% and it's currently in production at a dozen sites. He took my references and assured me he was going to consider our proposal carefully. I shared our research on Crystal Power with him—he got a little defensive. I assured him I wasn't being negative, but I felt obligated to point out the risk was considerable!

This morning I got a call and Zeb says he has chosen Crystal Power because they are the future leaders in our industry. I am devastated!"

"Lloyd I want you to do some homework for me this evening. First, tell me what you learned from this experience. Then, I want you to make a list of the executives you spoke with at Howard Brothers about the S6000. See you at 8 am sharp!"

"Sir, I was out sold plain and simple," Lloyd began. *"Since Zeb was the VP of Engineering, I didn't speak with anyone else, which was probably my second mistake!"*

"Lloyd, you made several mistakes beyond those two; but, before you beat yourself up too badly, grab a tie and meet me at my car. We have a lunch with Zeb and his boss, Ted Graves!"

The lunch was cordial, although Zeb was clearly a bit uncomfortable. Lloyd's sales manager was in fine spirits and seemed to be enjoying the small talk. Finally, he turned the conversation to business.

"I understand you've selected a UV Fluxtron for your new green building. Gutsy move, but we wish you the best! Just one comment to correct though...the process is not yet patented. The application has been filed, but not yet approved. Our guys are looking at the science behind it and, surprisingly enough, are skeptical."

Zeb and his boss laughed.

"Ted, I want you to know if the delivery of your unit doesn't work out, or you have other problems, I'll personally do everything I can to get you a replacement S6000 off the line on short notice. You're an important customer and we respect your decision!"

Graves was a conservative manager who had complete responsibility for operations. It was his job to worry about 'what ifs' and he took the responsibility seriously. His face reflected a trace of anxiety.

The ride back to the office was long and uncomfortable for Lloyd. The cell phone interrupted their sports discussion. His manager thanked Ted for making time for lunch and added, *"Actually we're projecting the wait time for an S6000 to be about 120 days from order. I think you should be concerned! I suggest we deliver a unit to Vermont—strictly, as a back up for the UV Fluxtron. Thank you, Sir, Lloyd will have the order on Zeb's desk for signature tomorrow!"*

Mr. Graves had decided buildings in Vermont, without reliable heat, could be cold in the winter.

PERIPHERALS

The Definition:

Peripheral competitors appear periodically as adversaries. They are either tactical (opportunistic) or strategic (expansionist) challengers.

Opportunistic competitors are focused on finding opportunity wherever it presents itself. Their mindset is simply: any opportunity is a good opportunity. Their product, with a minimum of required features and functions might be attractive to a potential purchaser. It may represent a temporary fix to an immediate need. Usually, the attractiveness is tied to price, delivery terms or a realization that the need is not currently a priority business issue. *"This product can get us by for now!" "It does enough to meet our needs."* Buyers will entertain a new competitor into a niche out of dissatisfaction with the current choice of vendors, or because they have developed a personal relationship with an opportunistic seller.

Here is an example: An unknown vendor of inexpensive consumer nail guns is invited to bid a proposal against the industrial Gold Standard. Why? The prospect's budget is extraordinarily tight. The new vendor may meet the minimum product requirement short term and temporarily resolve the management's financial problem.

Expansionist competitors are testing potential new markets. They are attempting to gain experience, make business judgments and secure a foothold. How their product fits in this new market may become an initial, temporary or ongoing challenge.

Initially, expansionists present products that are incomplete. They will then attempt to increase their robustness. Their solution may have been specially tailored to adjacent or unrelated markets where you seldom compete. The product could be the Gold Standard in its own marketplace, and this challenger may be a substantial enterprise.

Successful expansionists strategically ask:

- Can we sell this product outside our current niche?
- How can we best secure several test accounts?
- Can we dominate the new marketplace?
- Will this market meet our profit objectives?

All Peripheral competitors deserve careful scrutiny and aggressive responses. Remember, by its very nature, competition is expansionary.

The path to growth for many organizations is to find new markets to sell into, either on a temporary or long-term basis. Don't allow them to get comfortable exploring your marketplace!

Their Goal:

Enter into a new market. The opportunity may be viewed either as a tactical sale of product to an unanticipated prospect or a strategic foray.

Competitive Strengths:

1. They may be successful businesses with expansionary ambitions and the ability to execute.
2. The product may have a strong following in its niche and be adaptable.
3. They may, initially, be willing to buy business as an entry point.

Competitive Weaknesses:

1. Peripherals could be businesses struggling to find a market or sales.
2. They may not understand either the marketplace or prospect needs.
3. The commitment and resources to enter the marketplace and compete may not be fully known or sustainable.
4. They may not succeed with the product or positioning as a competitor.

Their Selling Message and Competitive Positioning:

The selling message will tell you the true extent of the competitive threat. When a Peripheral positions itself as a successful business, in an expansionary stage, looking for adjacent or compatible niches, you have a challenger. The reveal statement will also reinforce the strength and expertise they can bring to a new market. They will offer verifiable reference accounts and often ask the prospect to serve as a partner in this new opportunity. The prospect will in return receive special treatment and significant benefits.

Opportunistic entrants will start by claiming, *"You should be able to use our product just like everyone else!"* The selling message will not convey special marketplace expertise. In fact, the uniqueness of the niche will be ignored or glossed over in favor of general business knowledge. Their approach will be to generally ignore the opposition. These entrants want to make an opportunistic sale and move on.

Why They Win Business:

A decision maker is willing to chance they can transition a market and/or adopt their product. Taking a chance is often the result of dissatisfaction with the product solutions currently available, or the extension of a personal relationship. Occasionally, the decision maker views the need for the product or specific features as minimal and will choose any vendor offering special concessions.

Rebutting Peripherals:

1. **Make Peripherals work hard for the business!** This action sends a message to a potential expansionist and will not be lost on a tactical opportunist: you will not cede your prospects easily!
2. **Question if the product really meets the prospect's needs.** Partial solutions are sometimes more costly then the original problem they claim to fix. I refer to this as unintended consequences. Problem 'A' is resolved, but 'B' is created and it's more costly than 'A' was!
3. **Reiterate your belief that industry expertise and your market focus are valuable and essential to the prospect's long-term success.**
4. **Ask prospects to consider what happens if Peripheral decides to abandon the market for any number of legitimate business reasons?** What impacts will that decision have on customers? Suppose Peripheral cannot find any other customers? Tough questions you will want to ask your prospects to consider.

CASE STUDY
Competing With Peripherals

"David, we're going to look at Weir International before we commit to your proposal."

"Who? I'm sorry I have never heard of Weir, and I've spent the last 10 years selling fixed-asset management software to colleges and universities. I have honestly never come across these people!"

The prospect just smiled. *"Actually, they're very big in the insurance industry. I used them at my last job and I suspect they could easily meet the needs of this University. Great company, people and product!"*

So ended David's introductory call with the newly appointed comptroller. He swallowed hard and muttered, *"I should have known this account was too good to continue the way it has for the last several years."* Worst yet, his boss was really counting on Midwest State for a quick year-end decision; this was now going to be more complicated then David had anticipated.

"Who?" was also his boss' response. *"Find out everything you can about Weir and call me Sunday evening. I have to catch my flight, got to go. David, you told me this sale was a slam-dunk. What happened?"*

His prospect was correct; Weir was a highly successful player in the commercial insurance software market. They offered a broad line of financial and accounting products. There was not a single educational institution on the web site reference list.

Peter Hamel was excited about his promotion to Business Development. His mission at Weir was to open the education market for their financial software suite of products. Peter was given six months to penetrate the education market or move on to another opportunity. Selling to the insurance vertical had been his vocation for the last few years, but it was clear his sales territory and those of many of his colleagues were heavily penetrated. A new industry was just what the business needed. His networking paid handsome dividends when he discovered a Weir customer was now the Comptroller at Midwest State.

Bob French was feeling overwhelmed! A new job in a completely new environment like Midwest State–change was not his forte. The idea of once again doing business with a top-flight vendor like Weir was a real source of comfort. He was sure the software would easily accommodate the education business; after all, fixed assets were all pretty much the same. How different could it possibly be? He believed Weir could quickly resolve any missing functionality issues.

David was taken back by the reaction his manager had to Weir. *"Make sure we win this deal. If you miss your forecast date, okay, but more importantly, we do not want our niche to be compromised by this competitor! If they win this opportunity, they'll be on their way to becoming an established challenger."* David started to think about who he needed to call at Midwest State and his strategy for winning the order.

The message from Bob French was very clear. *"I have decided on Weir, and I hope you will respect the decision and withdraw."*

David was fully expecting this news and had carefully

thought out his response. *"Are you truly certain this product will meet your needs? My experience with the university is they are not much for taking risk."* The plea barely drew a response. *"Suppose Weir can't gain traction in this market, where does that leave you?"* French was resolute. *"Don't we get any credit for our expertise in this industry and our relationship with Midwest?"* Again the questions fell on deaf ears.

"David, I have made my mind up, the risk is minimal, I'm comfortable all fixed assets are essentially the same, this is not important enough to fight about...give it up!"

David knew he was about to escalate the stakes, but he was not going to let Weir into his account without a true struggle! Stopping this transaction was worth the controversy he was about to unleash.

"I'm disappointed to hear this, but really shocked that I have never been given the opportunity to present my product to the full finance committee. The Weir solution is clearly missing features the University will need! Every other sale we competed for at this University was always predicated on a formal presentation and full committee review and approval. I don't understand why you're changing the standard process? Especially when the competitor's product is fraught with unknown risks."

David had put Bob French in an awkward position. His allies had carefully coached him and the result was as they predicted—gridlock.

Rumor quickly circulated that a formal protest would be forthcoming. David's personal contacts were working overtime to prevent this transaction. In fact, the general consensus within the finance group was embarrassment over the shabby treatment David had received.

There was also a sense the new comptroller had learned a much needed lesson about how things were done at Midwest. *"We don't take unnecessary risks with new products nor do we change vendors without good reason."*

Peter was incredulous. *"I can't understand how this competing salesperson can stop your decision!"*

French was frustrated and it showed. *"I didn't realize the extent of the formal procedure I had to go through to purchase something this insignificant...nor did I realize how well connected your competitor is. The project is going to be delayed at least six months, and I'll have to follow a formal evaluation process."*

French knew, in time, he might build a consensus for the Weir product, but that was a challenge for a later date.

David described the situation to his boss as both good news and bad news. *"Weir didn't win the order, but neither did I!"*

Peter had little time to waste. Midwest was finished for the foreseeable future and his clock was ticking.

Sometimes victory comes in a form you least expect.

BRAND NEW

The Definition:

New companies are created every business day. They may have seasoned owners, managers with familiar names in an industry. They may be unknowns with little or no business experience. A business niche often determines how frequently new entrants appear. Industries with high barriers to entry or significant capital requirements will not see Brand New as frequently as the service or consumer-oriented marketplaces. The reality of competition is Brand New entrants are always seeking business opportunities they can lay claim to.

Their Goal:

Entrants aspire to become Mainstream or The Next Big Thing, while others with greater ambition want to achieve Gold Standard status. In reality, Brand New will become one of the six other types of competitors we've explored if they can survive the first several years of existence. Establishing one or several marquee accounts is the first order of business.

Competitive Strengths:

1. They may have discovered a way to create, reinvent or invigorate a marketplace. Perhaps, they'll offer a new product or service to a community. The most successful will be change agents, rather than 'me-too' providers.
2. They have a large dose of motivation, energy, flexibility and a desire for success at creating a new business, in the face of real obstacles.
3. The weakness, indifference or inconvenience of existing competitors becomes their strength.
4. They offer businesses and consumers additional choice. This is especially valuable in markets replete with Peripherals and Bottom Feeders.

Competitive Weaknesses:

1. They must overcome the challenge of delivering value, acquiring customers, and establishing a viable business model that results in cash flow and profits.
2. They will inevitably have to manage the business to overcome the unexpected and unanticipated.
3. The failure rate of new ventures is significant—a fact that is not lost on prospects and customers.

Their Selling Message and Competitive Positioning:

We are new! We believe we can do it better, cheaper and quicker than the competition! The 'better' may be a new product, service or evolutionary enhancement. The message will announce: *"The cure for the common cold!"* or the enhanced benefit of *"Thirty percent more adhesive power than Gold Standard can provide!"*

Even the most mundane of Brand New will have some claim to filling a void that the competition has not responded to: *"We are open until midnight seven days a week!"* ... *"Our store is the only grocer within 20 miles of the Route 1 intersection!"*

Why They Win Business:

Decision makers are sometimes drawn to new entrants because they offer a unique product. Often, they simply have earned the chance to replace a failed vendor. Some businesses will make concerted efforts to find and support new business ventures.

Rebutting Brand New:

1. **They are new!** New equals risk, which in many markets will discourage both consumers and businesspeople charged with the responsibility of purchasing.
2. **Remind the audience new means a clean slate only temporarily.** When the euphoria fades, the reality of delivering value, providing customers with service and support begin to come into focus. Then you can observe how well Brand New has performed. Remember, performance will either validate or terminate Brand New!
3. **Turn the challenge of new competition into an opportunity to rethink, refine and focus your business.** Ask yourself what they see that you have not? What can you do to improve your business? Create a strategy to build real barriers to discourage new competitors, before they enter your space.

CASE STUDY
Competing With Brand New

Brian Edwards knew how to throw one heck of a party, which is why he landed the senior position in the Corporate Events Department several years ago. He always marveled that serious business people would actually pay him to spend their money for them. As much as he enjoyed his assignment, he also realized his employers wanted first-class results from each and every event. The location of corporate headquarters in a small Midwest community was a real challenge. Quality caterers were hard to come by.

"Look, here's the bottom line—your catering service is not very good lately. The menu hasn't changed, the quality is down and you were late in setting up at two major meetings last month." Brian knew from the blank stare he was getting the owner just didn't get his message.

"I can't do any better than I can do!" was the terse reply. Brian couldn't help laughing to himself. The thought of firing yet another caterer was more than he could deal with today. How many more of these people will I fire, before I am reduced to recruiting high school students from Home Economics classes?

He returned to his desk to get yet another terse message from the CEO's administrative assistant, *"Bill is complaining about the food again, and he wants to see you next week about the spring event schedule, it looks to be quite heavy...call me."*

Margo had responded to his advertisement for catering services. The letter was well written and organized; but now, sitting here in his office, she looked to be very young—much too young to be running her own business.

"Actually I am younger than I look and far less experienced!" Brian could not help but smile from ear to ear.

Her demeanor was polite, although a look of intensity was written on her face. *"I started working in restaurants at 13; by 15, I was a line cook; and at 17, I ran the lunch shift. Someday, I'll be a top-draw chef and entrepreneur, but for now, I'd like a chance to cater for your business!"*

The biggest surprise was yet to come when Brian asked about her business. She reached into a brief case and extracted a typed document. *"What's this?"*

"Mr. Edwards, it's a business plan with a list of the equipment I will need, and, of course, how I intend to pay back your initial investment!"

When he regained his composure, he thanked her for her time and walked her to the office door.

"You may think the proposal is silly; but, you also should feel free to call me, and at least, try my service for one single event."

The CEO, Bill Campo, was really enjoying Brian's rendition of his latest caterer's interview. *"Wow, you have to really respect someone who has that kind of courage. We need more people around here with her spunk! Who knows, maybe she can really cater an event?"*

Desperate times call for desperate measures Brian thought, *"Margo, I have a luncheon for about 15 customers next Thursday. I will advance you the money to get the food and to rent equipment. I have to hear from you by tomorrow morning."*

Margo was already in the building lobby when he arrived at 8 am.

Frank was in damage control mode. He had been sloppy with this account and he knew it, but he was still better than this new competitor. He had seen other caterers come and go, he lost accounts, found new ones and the business went on. He was going to fight to keep this major account!

"Come on...Brian, you replaced me with some kid? I've been doing this for 15 years. Okay, we've had some problems, but they're fixed. I'm not perfect, but I know what I'm doing. Anybody can get lucky once!"

The CEO's administrative assistant reminded Brian: *"Bill is asking if Margo can cater the Board lunch next week?"* Brian was astute; he could sense the difference between a question and a command. *"I will make the arrangements, but don't hold me responsible if she gives a presentation about her business plan while she's catering lunch!"*

Over the next several weeks, Margo's assignments became more frequent. Her performance was consistently good, but it was difficult to tell how she'd perform on a big stage supervising a larger staff.

The flagship event for Brian was the annual company sponsored golf tournament. Hundreds of customers, prospects and VIP's attended. The event included a dozen catered events and a gala dinner. Frank and Margo both were invited to meet with the corporate event team and present their proposals.

Frank was focused on winning this project. He presented his proposal in a relaxed confident manner, *"I have already twice proven I can do this event, but I am committed to doing it even better this year. I have some new menu ideas in addition to my most popular cuisine. You can rest assured I'll get this job done, so you can concentrate on other more important issues."*

The committee was clearly skeptical. One member summed up the frustration. *"We know you can do this job, the question is will you really give us your best, or just do what is necessary to get by? We were waiting to hear something extraordinary...instead, I'm getting the impression this is more of the same."*

A supporter reminded the group, *"Let's not get too far out on the limb here, Frank knows what we want."*

Frank closed his proposal with a simple statement, *"I am offering you something extraordinary! I can and will give you a better performance and I will do it at the same price as last year, $500,000. I guarantee better performance, flat cost and no surprises!"*

A committee member remarked, *"If you had been this responsive a year ago, we wouldn't be looking at replacing you!"* The remark was not lost on Frank who knew he had created this competition.

Margo's approach was creative and it fit her image. *"If you want more of the same—choose my competitor. If you want to make this a memorable tournament, one your guests will remember and talk about all year, then give me one thing and one thing only...the gala dinner! I will give you an evening to remember! My competitor can handle all the other events; I want the piece de resistance! Turn to Page 1 in your handouts, and we'll go through my suggestions..."*

The presentation was an answer to the 'extraordinary' challenge and changed the playing field.

"How can we be sure you can pull this off?" The room was silent and hung on her response.

"You can't be sure, but I can assure you I have as much at stake as you. I'm willing to work for nothing more than my direct costs. I propose you get together as a committee after the event; and if you believe I exceeded your expectations, pay me what you believe is a fair profit. I will trust you to do the right thing, just as you will have to trust me!"

The committee debated and finally reached a conclusion...

It was a cold fall afternoon. *"Just one last event and I'm done!"* Relocation had grown increasingly attractive for Brian; landing a job as General Manager of a large new tropical resort property would be the end of his days in the snow. He chuckled and recalled meeting Margo over twelve years ago. *"I never would have guessed the highlight of my career would be giving her a start!"*

The airport manager tapped him on the shoulder, *"Her Gulfstream is about ten minutes out. Not every day we have an honest-to-gosh celebrity visiting this city! Look at all the press! Did you really give her...her first break, just like she always mentions on TV?"*

Brian responded, "I did! My reward is a new job in the Caribbean and calling her—Boss!"

BOTTOM FEEDERS

The Definition:

Bottom Feeders are market share laggards who exist in every competitive arena. They may have questionable products, be financially distressed, operate the business poorly, and fail miserably at providing customer service. Each one or several of these problems may apply!

Bottom Feeders are constantly on the verge of extinction. Survival from week to week is nothing new! Even worse, they will do any and everything imaginable to win business. It's this very need to survive that often makes them so dangerous.

Their Goal:

Continuance of the business! Ultimately, they may work towards discovering a way to execute market share growth and fixing their deficiencies.

Competitive Strengths:

1. With little to lose, and driven to survive, they can be both aggressive and, at times, creative marketers.
2. They appeal best to prospects primarily driven by a special circumstance or price concessions.
   "I know they are terrible, but the store is never crowded."
   "At this price, I'll buy from anyone!"
3. They may have enough name recognition to be tacitly accepted within their marketplace.
   "This product is not important enough to worry about purchasing it from..."

Competitive Weaknesses:

They have one or many serious business flaws! That's the reason they lag in market share. The weakness may vary from one Bottom Feeder to another, but it is present.

Their Selling Message and Competitive Positioning:

Bottom Feeders often subscribe to the old adage: *A good offense is the best defense.* They will attempt to keep the companies they are competing against on the defensive; making derogatory statements such as:

- *The product The Next Big Thing offers has a lot of problems!*
- *Gold Standard is losing its best people; something's going on over there!*
- *A prospect once remarked, "I cannot get them to stop telling me negative things about your company. I also cannot get them to tell me why I should buy their product, other than yours is a mess!"* A classic Bottom Feeder.

Bottom Feeders are not alone in the use of negative selling. They are, however, the only profile which embraces the practice as a strategy. When they must focus on their own product or business, the message will be quick and simple. *"We offer a good product at a competitive price."* They realize that it's difficult to paint an exciting picture of a business that has a poor market share position.

The mindset of the organization embraces the selling message that has worked best—continuous, ongoing negative attacks against the competition. The more they fear a particular competitor, the more vitriolic the attacks will be. Any and everything becomes fair game when reality and truthfulness endanger their survival.

Bottom Feeders are most effective when they sell commodity products. Pencils do not require service, support or a vendor with large amounts of competence to be valuable, whereas, building a nuclear power plant does!

Why They Win Business:

The transaction is driven by a special consideration, which outweighs all the other concerns. *"At this price who cares!" or "I'm not waiting two weeks for a alternative, this will do!"*

Rebutting Bottom Feeders:

1. **Disclose to your prospects that Bottom Feeders may focus on nega-**

tive selling. *"It is embarrassing, but it's how they choose to do business."*

2. **Encourage the prospect account to insist that each competitor sell his or her value in a positive professional manner.** I have found that candidly discussing a simple reality can really focus a prospect. "*After you make your selection, all that will matter is the company and product you have chosen. The attainment of real value will be between you and your vendor. Make sure you really know the product and your business partner, because you may be betting your company and position on the outcome.*"
3. **Disclose the facts—Bottom Feeder has a 2% market share!** Let the prospect figure out why or ask for your opinion.
4. **Do not get drawn into a negative slugfest.**

CASE STUDY
Competing With Bottom Feeders

"I can't believe the price quote Global Construction came in with for this project!" Robby complained.

"I can...they believe being large gives them the right to ask for premiums many business owners are not going to tolerate. Their work is really nothing special. Let's go through my proposal one more time."

Dan sensed he had an ideal prospect. Obviously price sensitive and perhaps willing to sacrifice quality to get what he wanted. He remembered his sales manager's advice: people want cheap construction, they just don't want it called that or to admit to it. Just be polite, and keep attacking the competition—a good offense is the best defense!

Robby was in a crunch; Winter Harbor Marine & Supply had been in his family for three generations. Robby often wondered if his business would not have been better off without all the new boaters who suddenly discovered Winter Harbor. He badly needed to expand his marina's boat warehouse and parts inventory, but he didn't have enough capital. His customers were vocalizing their unhappiness with his constant shortage of parts and the annual boat storage crunch. The business was suffering, and it was clear he needed to change or risk losing everything. Two new competitors with modern facilities had begun taking his customers.

The local bank was willing to finance his expansion, but that was a very big leap of faith for someone who was schooled never to borrow. If he had to finance, he was determined to avoid any extravagances. The challenge had become defining what was extravagant.

Robby's son, RJ, would soon inherit the business, and he had a different view of expanding. *"We have a long history of being the marina of choice, and our location is simply the best. We need to leverage ourselves financially and reclaim our dominance!"*

Maritime Solutions, Dan's employer, had a checkered track record of construction practices. They minimally built to code, cut corners whenever possible, but survived by offering low prices. Dan was not pleased to find RJ was joining Robby for their lunch meeting.

"Dan, you sure have the lowest bid on this project, but I have some real concerns about how you have put this proposal together," RJ began. *"I gave the drawings to a colleague, who's an architect, and asked him for a complete review. Are you available to answer his questions?"*

Dan was beginning to get angry with RJ. He was convinced the Global sales team was behind this interference.

"RJ, I've been through this with your Dad. We build smart, we build quickly, and we don't pad the jobs with red tape or unnecessary overhead. Our jobs are finished before Global figures out who's in charge of one of the projects. It's why we beat them whenever we really want a contract. They are big, slow and expensive. Heck, the new Civic Center they built was way over budget. The new sports area, have you seen that mess? Just awful construction! I can re-bid your job with more drawings and details, but all that will accomplish is to raise the price and waste everybody's time. We need to start now to get this done before the winter storage season!"

The walk back to the marina was contentious. Robby respected his son's acumen and MBA, but he could not get past the cost issue.

"Dad, I can cover the cost differential with better financing arrangements. Let's not build something we're going to regret, especially since it will be my problem long after you retire! We have a dinner tonight with the team from Global Construction, so please, just keep an open mind—okay?"

The sales executives from Global were focused on the benefits they were prepared to offer. They never attacked the competition. The dinner meeting was about discovering what they could do to assist Robby and RJ to make a favorable decision.

"Robby, we need to do some work to get you comfortable with the cost we have proposed. Just remember, the initial outlay for the warehouse is just part of the complete cost to your business over the next 20 years. The proposed facility is energy efficient, uses solar power for heat-

ing and is essentially maintenance free. Every one of our buildings comes with a full five-year warranty."

Robby finally asked, *"I keep hearing a lot of comments about the problems your company has run into, what's going on?"*

The senior executive laughed, *"Robby, I run into the same question every time we compete with 'You Know Who'...the bottom line is, we have given you references; and we'll stand by our track record. I wish our competitor would talk more about his product and not waste your time with negative comments about mine. Unfortunately, it's how they choose to do business."*

RJ finally reached a point of exasperation with Dan. *"I don't want to hear any more advice or comments about Global. I want to go through the specifications step-by-step so our architect fully understands your design. This project is too important and too costly to leave the details for a later date. Dan, if you can't resolve these questions, we're just going to eliminate your proposal. By the way, I'll need some additional references."*

Dan had already tuned the conversation out. He was thinking about his prospect list and who best represented his next opportunity.

Seven distinct competitors...
each with a different strategy to achieve the same goal...
win business at your expense!

Competition is not just about putting your best efforts forward; it's about dramatically improving the odds of winning a new customer. Profiling Seven Competitors identified each specific challenger and provided insights into how each adversary will attempt to win orders. We also clearly defined what you can and should do to prevail!

In our next chapter, we'll explore the specific match-ups that are most advantageous, as well as the most difficult. Competing effectively requires you to decide who you want to compete with, and who to avoid. Remember, you want to compete against adversaries you can prevail over again-and-again!

TEST YOUR KNOWLEDGE

1. List the seven types of competitors.

....

....

2. Competitors are not created equal. They each have different needs and approaches to winning. **True/False**

3. The following applies to Gold Standard...

- ❑ Well known and respected for their achievement;
- ❑ Viewed as thought leaders in their market;
- ❑ Both of the above;
- ❑ Neither of the above.

4. When competing with Gold Standard...

- ❑ Turn their sales and account plans upside down.
- ❑ Take them on at every opportunity.
- ❑ Stay away from their customer base.
- ❑ Work only as hard as they do.

5. Momentum players who have gained market share and visibility are known as.. .

6. Mainstream competitors seek to achieve more modest goals. They will not bet the business on highly leveraged growth plans. **True/False**

7. What's an outstanding strength of Mystic competitors?

....

Name one weakness.

....

8. What are the two types of Peripheral competitors?

.... & ....

9. Peripheral competitors are periodic adversaries. **True/False**

10. What's the biggest challenge Brand New must overcome?

....

CHAPTER 4

Favorable And Difficult Competitive Matches

I am sure many of you are already thinking, *"Is my business represented by one of the profiles?"* The answer is YES! The profiles apply to your own business. We each own or work for one of the competitive profiles, and it's important to understand which applies! How do Mystics best position against Gold Standard? Should Bottom Feeders compete with The Next Big Thing? It's impossible to answer these questions until you understand the profile you represent.

Know your Opponent and Know Yourself!

Assessing your own profile requires a strong dose of reality. I always chuckle when an executive tells me that they're the Gold Standard of their marketplace. Trust me on this, a business with gross annual sales of $10,000 is not likely to be the Gold Standard of anything–Brand New, yes; Mainstream, maybe; but not, Gold Standard!

Business decisions based on tomorrow's dreams rather than today's reality can lead to serious consequences. I sincerely believe you can become whatever you dream of being. Unfortunately, the inability to recognize your competitive profile can lead to poor decisions and ultimately failure.

What's the reason so many small business ventures fail within the first three years? Owners and staff extract a steep toll when they begin spending capital and time chasing low-probability opportunities. Purchasing excess inventory and hiring employees in anticipation of future sales revenue, creates an enormous financial burden and seals the fate of the business.

The vast majority of businesses grow stage by stage over their lifespan. Gold Standard and The Next Big Thing are not created overnight, but through challenging and often difficult years of growth. Many new entrepreneurs are astonished when they realize the road to success is long and difficult. Reality may tell you that your business is currently a Brand New or a Mainstream. That doesn't mean you will always fit this profile; with a good business plan and smart execution, you may well become The Next Big Thing in your market!

When you're able to see reality,
you have the power to embrace change and to prosper.

Prevailing in a competitive contest, where the vast majority of business opportunities will be, requires understanding your profile and the competition's. Limited selling time is the great equalizer for many businesses.

Part of using selling time efficiently is to maximize the time you spend competing against those businesses you can easily prevail over, and limiting your efforts against those you don't fare well against. In fact, most salespeople have a competitor they know they just plain own! Sales careers and businesses often under perform because they waste extraordinary amounts of time, effort and money constantly competing with entities they can't prevail over, or where they have a low rate of success.

The path to competitive success is more effective if you select your opponents. Slaying dragons may be heroic, but it can also be painful and fatal!

I learned this lesson several years ago as the principal of a software company focused on providing applications that automated the commercial lending function. Our product was exclusively bundled with a hardware platform offered by a well-known vendor. Our partner who I'll refer to as 'A' was incredibly successful in beating vendor 'B' but a disaster when competing with company 'C' or 'D'. Our first year in business was spent accommodating our partner in their efforts to win accounts from C and D. They tried valiantly to use our application as valuable enhancement. We barely survived the experience! The second year, I only responded to requests to compete against vendor B. We were much less popular with our partner—but the results for our business were excellent and, I have little doubt, prevented us from failing as an enterprise.

Our partner was a Mainstream competitor; opponent B was a fading Mainstream; C and D, respectively, were Gold Standard and The Next Big Thing. We eventually switched partners and became closely aligned with the Gold Standard, a decision that allowed us to grow our sales and market recognition rapidly. Brand New partnered with Gold Standard was much more powerful than a similar deal with a Mainstream.

Will each profile exist in every market?

The simple answer is NO! In a new or emerging market, there may initially be only Brand New and Mystic players. As these markets evolve to maturity, Peripheral, Mainstream, and TNBT competitors will emerge. Mature markets will usually support the existence of a Gold Standard. Conversely, markets in the final stages of existence may have only Peripherals and Bottom Feeders left as challengers. The lifecycle of a marketplace will influence the types of competition that exist.

The creation of **The Competitor's Resume** will assist you in determining which profiles you are currently competing against. It will also give you the opportunity to reflect on what stage your market has reached in its lifecycle.

Will I compete with adversaries who have the same profile I have?
Just as every profile may not exist at a given time in the marketplace, you may find yourself in competition with other businesses fitting the same profile as your company. For example, Brand New competing with Brand New is very typical. Occasionally, a market will have two TNBT or several Mainstream competitors.

Use the profiles to remind yourself to focus on selling your competitive strengths and eliminating the competitive weakness issues your adversaries will attempt to exploit. Focus on your selling message and competitive positioning and rebut the message of the competition.

For example, Brand New is often criticized over its inability to transition to a mature organization supporting and servicing products and customers. Since you know this issue will be questioned, even by another Brand New, reveal how you plan to manage this challenge. The very fact you have addressed the concern, and have clearly given it careful consideration, will separate you from many of your profile peers. You have the knowledge to engage in proactive selling, which trumps the practice of just reacting to your adversaries!

What are the most favorable and the difficult match-ups for each profile?

GOLD STANDARD

The Best: Competing against Mainstream, Peripherals and Bottom Feeders allows for the continuance of a dominant market share. These competitors are in the sweet spot for Gold Standard. Brand New and Mystics are also very good match-ups if Gold can manage the sales process to its playbook. The power of the Gold Standard is evident from the breadth of the favorable opportunities they enjoy.

The Difficult: The Next Big Thing is the most significant challenge. The advantage of marketplace momentum, growing recognition, and a credible reference base all combine to make Gold Standard's natural advantage less significant. If TNBT can portray Gold as an outdated or under-performing solution, they will be formidable. Gold needs to label TNBT as a risk that should be avoided.

The Toss-Ups: Brand New and Mystics are capable of an occasional challenge. They must carefully position their company and product, while forcing Gold Standard to work outside of its comfort zone. They enter the competition as weakened versions of TNBT.

THE NEXT BIG THING

The Best: Peripherals, Mystics, Brand New and Bottom Feeders are easily overcome. Mystics and Brand New in particular will be viewed as early stage versions of TNBT without a record of success. Mainstream is a surmountable opponent, though the most challenging of this group.

The Difficult: Gold Standard is the core competitor. In order to overtake their market share and gain entry to a lucrative client base, TNBT needs to extend the momentum to winning new opportunities from Gold and converting its customer base.

The Toss-Ups: Mainstream can frustrate TNBT if they are an incumbent vendor or successfully positioned in select accounts. Some audiences will seek a safe alternative to a momentum player.

MAINSTREAM

The Best: Peripherals and Bottom Feeders are primary sources of competitive success. Mystics and Brand New entrants are within the domination zone, especially if the competition is over accounts that have an existing relationship with Mainstream.

The Difficult: The Gold Standard and The Next Big Thing are both very tough competitors. They each have the customer base and name recognition to offset the primary strength of Mainstream.

The Toss-Ups: Mystics and Brand New can be effective challengers. They are strongest when competing for new relationships and positioning Mainstream as a solution that, for a specific reason, has failed to gain market dominance.

MYSTICS

The Best: An innovator who wants to change the marketplace by providing a breakout new product or service offering. If their offering is viewed as a viable and working product, they can dominate Peripherals, Brand New and Bottom Feeders.

The Difficult: The Next Big Thing is often, at the root, a Mystic that's evolved into a momentum player. Gold Standard can position as a safe proven solution to a Mystic who is viewed as overreaching. Mainstream competitors can enjoy the same protective reasoning.

The Toss-Ups: Mystics rise and fall based on their ability to deliver a product that works as touted. If that reality can't be demonstrated, they will struggle to prevail over any competitor. *"Sounds great,* ***but*** *has anyone verified the product performs as promised?"*

PERIPHERALS

The Best: The Opportunist's competitive focus should be on dominating Brand New and Bottom Feeders. Mystics can be a solid competitive match if they can be faulted for failing to deliver on promises of either product or service.

Expansionists compete well with each profile if they focus on offering strategic partnerships and special concessions to the prospect. The challenge is ultimately to evolve into at least a Mainstream competitor with a recognizable market share.

The Difficult: Gold Standard, The Next Big Thing, and Mainstream will win the preponderance of contests. They offer the safety and depth of deliverable commitments that Opportunistic Peripherals struggle to provide.

The Toss-Ups: Opportunists can place Mainstream in jeopardy if they have failed to satisfy their customers, or suffer from reputation issues.

BRAND NEW

The Best: Each and every new customer and order is a struggle. These new entrants must carefully choose their battles. Bottom Feeders,

Peripherals, Mystics and other Brand News are the better targets. In truth, no competitor is going to be easy for Brand New to dominate. They compete best when they provide for an unfulfilled market need or offer an alternative to an unpopular competitor or product.

The Difficult: Gold Standard, The Next Big Thing, and Mainstream are all extraordinarily difficult. Positioning as an alternative to well-established marketplace incumbents requires a large dose of creativity, flexibility and the willingness to compromise in order to win.

The Toss-Ups: Mainstream can be attacked successfully if they fail to satisfy their customers or suffer from reputation issues. Mystics are in play if they are proposing a non-verifiable product.

BOTTOM FEEDERS

The Best: There are very few sure opportunities to prevail against. Peripherals and Brand New present the most favorable, if any, matches. Bottom Feeders are relegated to working on the margins to pick up any business they can find.

The Difficult: Every sale is difficult! It should be no surprise that the business failure rate for Peripherals, Brand New and Bottom Feeders is much higher than the three competitors with strong market shares (Gold Standard, TNBT and Mainstream).

The profiles reflect a powerful reality—
The further removed from a dominant market share a business finds itself, the more challenging its competitive position.

The first part of ***Winning Business from Difficult Competitors*** has presented the initial steps to improving your competitive performance and advancing towards a dominant market share.

- Identify the competition and thoroughly examine the critical parts of their business, products and strategies.
- Ascertain the profile of each competitor and your own current profile.
- Learn the best methods for competing with each profile.
- Invest your time and money in those competitive contests you have the greatest chance to win.

A sustainable competitive advantage begins to emerge.

TEST YOUR KNOWLEDGE

1. The path to competitive success is more effective if you select your opponents. True/False

2. Sales reps and businesses often under-perform because they waste extraordinary amounts of time competing where they have a low rate of success or can't prevail. True/ False

3. The further removed from a dominant market share position a business is, the better its competitive position. True/False

4. Who's the most difficult challenger to Gold Standard?

....

5. The core competitor for TNBT is...
   - ❑ Mystics.
   - ❑ Brand New.
   - ❑ Bottom Feeders.
   - ❑ Gold Standard.

6. Mainstream's most difficult competitors are...
   - ❑ Peripherals and Bottom Feeders.
   - ❑ Gold Standard and TNBT.
   - ❑ Mystics and Brand New.
   - ❑ None of the above.

7. One thing you can be certain of is that each type of competitor profile will exist in every market. True/False

8. The inability to recognize your company's competitive profile is a competitive strength. True/False

9. As a business evolves, its profile will change. True/False

10. In some markets, your competitors may have the same profile as your business. True/False

The People Who Influence Competitive Choices

CHAPTER 5

The Selling Pyramid

Hand-in-hand with the challenge of competition comes the realization that it's left to people, whom we shall refer to as decision makers, to decide the outcome of our competitive struggle. People who exemplify the very best and worst of human nature.

Which is it? Decision makers are smart, witty and wonderful ladies and gentlemen. They behave rationally and make excellent decisions!
Or? Prospects are difficult, deceptive, and worst–they make decisions beyond belief and just plain stupid!

The truth is, unfortunately, both. This makes the act of competing for business complicated and difficult, as well as rewarding and exhilarating!

The second part of ***Winning Business from Difficult Competitors*** will explore who the decision makers in business enterprises really are, and equally important–what they need and why? We'll discuss why identifiable personality types have a predisposition to do business with organizations of a particular competitive profile.

Winning business is at the core of every successful enterprise. To whom you sell, and what message you deliver is crucial; just as crucial as recognizing and persuading decision makers to either act on or compromise their initial competitive preferences.

Although our attention is focused on these specific issues and the skills required to create competitive victories, learning to sell is a broader issue and outside the scope of this book. If you need to sharpen your sales skills, read the companion piece to this text, ***Smart Selling! Your Roadmap to Becoming a Top Performer***.

To whom should I sell?
What message should I deliver to that specific person?

Prevailing requires you to answer both questions. What's at stake?...the individual success of businessmen and women and, ultimately, their company's competitive growth and prosperity!

Have you ever calculated how much of your selling time is spent with people who cannot buy your product or service–even if they wanted to buy? How much effort is wasted on sales calls that result in polite rejections? *"Thanks for your time, we'll call you if we're interested?"* How many opportunities have been lost because you called on the wrong person, while the competition found the real decision makers? Many salespeople avoid confronting this topic because they know the answer is painful.

Selling time is truly finite; every wasted hour is an hour you cannot get back!

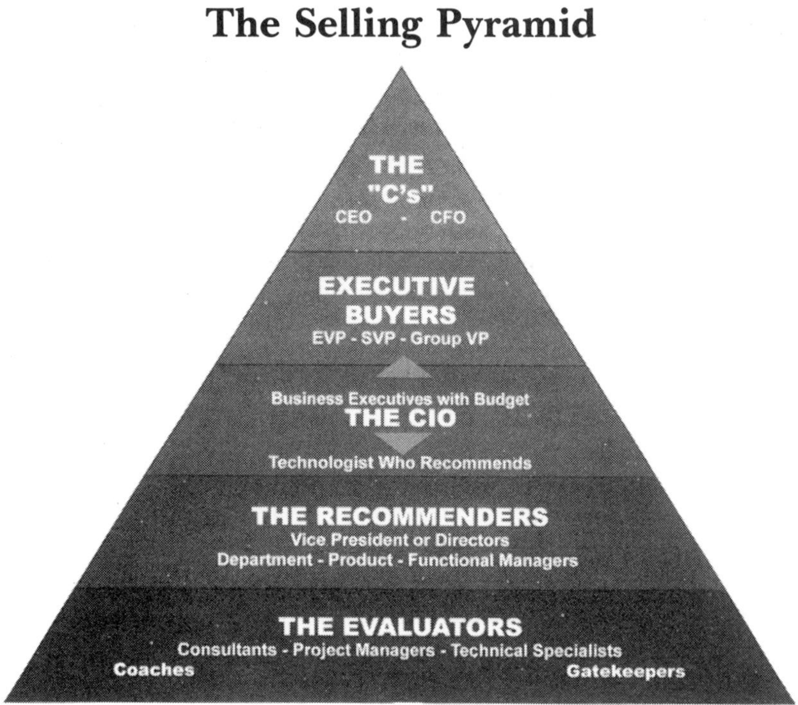

What is *The Selling Pyramid?*

The Selling Pyramid is the roadmap that points you right where you want to go to find decision makers! The vast majority of businesses are organized in some form of hierarchy. Recently, there has been a vigorous debate about the effectiveness of a hierarchical organization. The alternative is a collaborate approach to running a business. Both approaches have their merits and drawbacks. Many companies are a blend of both styles and often migrate back and forth from one form to the other.

However your prospect chooses to organize, you will find people assigned to the roles we're going to discuss. These roles will require the officeholder to work to a distinct set of needs in order to contribute and prosper in his or her assignment.

Why is finding decision makers paramount? First, by definition they're responsible for the strategic and tactical choices a business must make countless times each day. Second, they are empowered to turn decisions into action. Ultimately, they validate the success or failure of your competitive contests for business.

CEOs will have different needs than Project Managers and you need to understand those differences before you meet with either!

Unfortunately, far too many business people waste valuable opportunities failing to recognize and respond to this simple reality. This is not about manipulation; rather, it's about responding to the real needs that matter to each officeholder. Failure to meet the needs of the prospect's decision makers jeopardizes your competitive position.

I always remind readers there are three ways to deal with decision makers:

- Actively find and engage them in discussions about your product.
- Hope your competitors will mention you in their discussions.
- Just ignore them and hope for the best.

***The Selling Pyramid* is designed to help you understand the assignment and needs of your target audience. It will answer the question of what message to deliver and to whom.**

The Chiefs or Cs

The ultimate decision makers! They have the authority to act and the power to sustain their actions. Chief Executive Officers, the Chief Financial Officer and Chief Operating Officers are the senior managers you want to befriend and persuade. Smaller companies may use titles such as owner or managing partner. The larger your prospect's business, the more challenging it'll be to get an appointment. However, these executives aren't impossible to reach if you work smart!

Many pundits will tell you that to sell successfully in today's hyper-competitive markets you must sell to Cs. The truth is they are correct! What they don't tell you is that cold telephone calling, barrages of e-mails and snappy, clever headline letters have very low rates of success. Many of those techniques were far more viable in the 1990's when treasuries were overflowing, and almost any new product and service solution could be in vogue.

Today, operating expenses have been slashed time and again. In most businesses, the Cs have neither the time nor the interest to spend precious resources responding to the dozens of 'promised miracles' they receive each day. Many executives have capital to invest but are more cautious and discriminating about using it. Doing business with peers and known vendors matters because it's viewed as both safe and prudent.

If you are the senior officer in your company—pick up the phone! If you're not, your best leverage to a meeting will come through the senior executives in your company. Why? Cs love to network with peers. They understand the power of personal contacts...it's how the vast majority became Cs in the first place. Ask your CEO, or another senior executive officer, to contact the Cs at your prospect's firm for a meeting. Trust me on this, very few CEOs do not enjoy being asked and will relish the opportunity to assist you. The prospect's executives will respond to a direct contact from your executives before they'll entertain calls from yet another unknown sales representative. Company executives need to become regular contributors to the sales assignment.

Industry pundits, well-known consultants, academics, attorneys or business leaders are also great sources of introductions or referrals. Entrepreneurs and business owners will find this an excellent method to contact their peers at prospect accounts. Don't forget to ask your existing customers and reference accounts for their assistance! Introductions are important in a business environment that's under competitive stress.

The Cs are busy people, introductory meetings will be relatively short. Once you get your audience, here is what matters:

You must focus on what they need:

- **1st** **Profits**
- **2nd** **Increasing shareholder value**
- **3rd** **Growth of market share**
- **4th** **Their employees' welfare**
- **5th** **Their legacy, both public and personal.**

The Message you deliver must:

> **Reveal how your business and its product advances these specific needs!**

Answer their needs and you'll have a successful meeting. Unfortunately, the opposite is also true. A poor performance will hurt your efforts.

Competitors who can articulate why their product increases profits prevail! Contestants that can't or don't address the issue fail!

What are the most common causes of failure?

- Forgetting to focus on the five needs of all Cs.
- Not having a clear **Goal** for the meeting including an **Action** plan, and specific **Result** you want from the session.
- Appearing to be disorganized or 'just visiting'.
- Failing to listen carefully to and learn from the prospect.
- Offering a product that does not add value to the C's needs.

The CFO deserves special attention. He or she may be empowered to manage any and all capital expenditures with an iron fist. You may have to reach agreement with the CFO that your product's value meets whatever capital measurement criterion he or she employs. The sooner you understand the measurement hurdle and address it, the better your chance for success will be!

The Executive Buyers

The next power center on The Selling Pyramid is the Executive Buyer, with titles such as Executive Vice President, Senior Vice President, Group Vice President. Smaller companies use titles such as General Manager or Partner. They're responsible for one or several major functional areas, such as sales, marketing, engineering, manufacturing or operations. More importantly, they personally approve or control the final decisions on the vast majority of products and services. They own or control budgets and approve the funding of proposed expenditures.

Much like the Cs, to whom they typically report, they also have a busy schedule and a focus on, *"What can you do to help me?"* The vast majority aspires to be Cs and are well polished, political and driven to achieve those higher positions.

You must focus on what they need:

1st Growing revenues and/or their business unit profits

2nd Reducing expenses

3rd Increasing productivity

4th Enhancing their career aspirations and image.

The Message you deliver must:

Reveal how your business and its product advances these specific needs!

CASE STUDY
The Impact Of An Effective Message

Ernest had one meeting before his weekend respite. Friday was usually spent reviewing progress on the week's agenda items and any difficult personnel issues. This week included meetings with vendors proposing a new automated assembly line for his European manufacturing operation. The meetings were, at best, a disappointment. He couldn't help but wonder why the salespeople he met were so disorganized and continued to drag out a list of features he had little interest in. His staff had warned him to let them manage these visits and sort out the contenders.

Ernest had grown up in Sales before becoming Executive Vice President at Able Industries. No small accomplishment—Able was a global business with billions of dollars in revenue. He wanted to stay close to the project since it would immediately become a visible statement of personal success in his current assignment. It also had far reaching financial implications for the business.

Looking each sales executive in the eye was reassuring. Selecting carefully was important to him and the business. He still knew a thing or two about sales and enjoyed a good competitive tussle, but he was beginning to have his doubts...

Tim was a seasoned sales professional. He understood this initial call would be his one and only chance to convey a strong first impression. Calling on a very senior executive was an opportunity to advance his competitive position. He had carefully prepared for the meeting.

He had a preliminary list of issues to explore with his prospect and knew what commitments he intended to seek. Simple, right? He reminded himself to focus on the meeting's goal, take the actions to achieve it, and measure the results.

The call started with the usual pleasantries. Then, Tim went to work. *"Ernest, what do you need this project to accomplish?"* He listened closely to the answer Ernest offered. *"It sounds like reducing your cost structure is really the key. Did I understand that correctly? Does reducing cost include reducing the staff?"* Each response led to further discussion. *"Will you integrate the new assembly line with a just-in-time inventory control system? How quickly do you want to be in production?"* And finally, *"Who else are you considering for the project?"*

The questions were serious, focused and well thought out. Ernest quickly realized he had a knowledgeable and talented resource sitting in front of him. The conversation had immediately become a mutual exchange of information.

Tim proceeded, "*Our company has been very successful in helping large business enterprises just like Able Industries to create new automated assembly lines. I'm sure you know two of your competitors, Universal and Lawrence, are major customers. Let me take literally two minutes to tell you about our business. I believe we can prove our system will reduce your current cost structure, increase your productivity and integrate with your existing operating platforms. The results will translate into increased profits for the European operation. The task will require time and effort on both of our parts—if we can help, it will benefit both of our companies.*"

With a straight face, Ernest asked, *"Don't you want to tell me all about your best features?"* then chuckled.

"I can do that if you wish. I'd rather leave that for our next meeting after we have a broader understanding and agreement of the complete needs of your business."

"Tim, what do you propose for our next meeting?"

Tim just happened to have an image of the agenda clearly set in his mind.

Ernest shook Tim's hand and remarked, "*Thanks for visiting, I really enjoyed our discussion. I am looking forward to our next meeting and getting to know you!*" Ernest reflected later, *"Smart guy...good meeting."*

The quicker you find and engage the Executive Buyer, the more efficient and successful the selling effort will become. Far too many salesmen and saleswomen avoid the very audience that can and will decide the fate of their proposal.

Three principles to remember:

- People buy from people! Executive Buyers always have time for people that can help them achieve success.
- A relationship with top executives in your account is leverage that you can use when you work with the Recommenders and Evaluators, who are always present.
- If you fail to engage the Executive Buyer, and your competitor does—they will possess an enormous advantage!

The act of getting a meeting with this busy group of people is even easier than securing an appointment with a C. The same basic principles we discussed a short while ago work even more effectively with this audience. Top performing salesmen and saleswomen have learned to focus on finding, contacting and working with Executive Buyers.

Marginally performing sales reps, or the inexperienced, will often fall into the trap of inventing or anointing Executive Buyers. The justification is: *"John is the senior project manager for this evaluation. He's much more powerful than his position would indicate."* or *"Jeanne will decide whether to buy or not; she's well connected in the company, on the fast track."*

My rule of thumb is simple: If your contact does not have a significant title or report directly to the Cs, the chances of him or her being an Executive Buyer are slim.

In our example, John may well be an Evaluator or a Recommender, especially if he is focused on asking about product features. Test John by asking him to introduce you to his boss. If his boss turns out to be a middle level manager, I can assure you that your Executive Buyer is still to be discovered!

A final note of encouragement: Executive Buyers are savvy business people. Salespeople who can meet their needs and provide value are viewed as important. Just remember what really matters to an Executive Buyer, then ask for an opportunity to assist them.

The Chief Information Officer or CIO

This position in The Selling Pyramid exists primarily in large businesses and is focused around technology products or services. The incumbents are divided between Executive Buyers and Recommenders. Their role will vary from company to company. CIOs who have the authority to purchase technology solutions function as Executive Buyers. Those who can only study and recommend technology products to other executives are, in fact, Recommenders.

Ask the Chief Information Officer if he or she owns the budget and authority to purchase, or if they sponsor products. The answer will clarify the role they fill.

The Recommenders

Recommenders are the men and women who use your product and will be directly affected by its impact. They'll have titles such as Vice President, Director or Manager. They are responsible for managing divisions, departments or business units with specific functions—Director of Customer Support, Vice President of Quality Control, or Manager of Investor Relations.

They are responsible for budgets, but will often need to get approval on how, and when, the budget is to be spent. Recommenders will have more discretion when the economy is strong and they're meeting profit goals. However, they're the first to be constrained when profits turn down. Products that are being reordered or are viewed to be basic commodities required for day-to-day business operations may be purchased directly by some Recommenders. Knowing the details of how your product works and the scope of its performance are important. You, or a member of your selling team, has to satisfy their need to ask questions and learn about the functions and features of your product.

Your personal credibility and your company's reputation are both issues this audience will explore. Why? Recommenders rely on your product to provide daily value. They will be the first to know if it does exactly what you have claimed it will do. The Cs and Executive Buyers hold Recommenders responsible for products that fail to perform. The assurance that any problems will be quickly and personally managed to resolution is important.

You must focus on what they need:

- **1st** **Detailed product functions and features**
- **2nd** **Department productivity**
- **3rd** **Security and comfort.**

The Message you deliver must:

Reveal how your business and its product advance these specific needs!

Understanding what Recommenders care about has a direct impact on your ability to compete successfully. The key point:

Recommenders cannot give you a final YES...but, they can say NO and sustain it!

When we focus on Executive Buyers and their needs, this does not mean we can ignore the prospect account's Recommenders. The vast majority of products and services will require selling at multiple levels in The Selling Pyramid. The wisdom is to engage each audience and satisfy their wants and needs.

Several years ago, I had a chance meeting with a very senior Executive Buyer of a long-standing customer in a busy airport lounge. His account was now the responsibility of a sister division; so, we had not seen each other in several years. I couldn't help noticing that he was clearly uncomfortable and having difficulty holding eye contact. After several minutes, I inquired, *"How are we doing with your account?"* He proceeded to tell me that they had recently chosen a competitor's product for an important new business application they were about to introduce. *"I really like your company, you've been great partners. However, my business line manager could not get answers to his questions. He was uncertain that your product had the functions we apparently required. I did not want to order him to select your company, and I didn't have the time to investigate the specifics personally."* He continued on to say, *" I even called the new division president to tell him that you were in jeopardy, but the questions never got resolved!"*

Cannot give the final YES...but, can sustain NO!
That is why we call them Recommenders!

The Evaluators

Unfortunately, this is a very popular audience. They are capable of consuming vast amounts of your time and resources. We're going to discuss two distinct types of Evaluators: **Gatekeepers** and **Coaches.**

All Evaluators have a primary mission:

- They are paid to get information, compile, sort, slice, dice and refine it; then get more material, collateral, references or gossip about your product, your company and your competitors. The details are paramount and they can never have too much!
- Their goal is to make sure that decisions are analytic and, by their standards, factually correct.

The challenge with all Evaluators is to understand their assignment and respond without losing sight of the bottom line...they do not buy products!

You must focus on what they need:

1st Collecting information

2nd The evaluation process

3rd Control.

The Message you deliver must:

Reveal how your business and its product advance these specific needs!

Gatekeepers

Early in my selling career, I did a major product presentation for a manufacturing firm in the Midwest. All the participants introduced themselves and their positions in the company. As I customarily did in those days, I started the meeting by asking the audience to tell me what they needed to learn from my presentation. What knowledge was essential for them to hear about during our session? Within seconds, a very angry looking gentleman rose to his feet and announced loudly enough for most of Illinois to hear, "*Stop! No you don't! We do not answer any more questions! You get to answer OUR questions, then the meeting will be over!*" I had met the ultimate Gatekeeper. The good news, and the bad news, is that most Gatekeepers are subtler and less verbal!

This is not a particularly sales-friendly audience. Titles include Business Analyst, Consultant, Project Manager, Procurement Specialist or Product Engineer. By their very nature, they want to restrict your access to other parts of The Selling Pyramid. It's common to be told "*Anybody who wants to do business with this company has to have my approval,*" or "*Please do not contact anyone else at our company, I will make the decision to consider your product!*"

So what are the goals we need to keep in mind when working with Gatekeepers?

- Polite, but...just the facts! They must get the key details about the product or service documented. Don't be drawn into a 'show me more' whirlpool by continually volunteering more and more material. Just make sure the product's best features and functions stand out and all questions get responses.
- Work The Selling Pyramid! The Gatekeepers may object to this, but do not succumb to their desire to control the sales environment. Use your selling team and executive management to open doors throughout the prospect account.
- Remember: People buy from people! The facts matter, details count, evaluations are important; but, in the end, the Recommenders and Executive Buyers will make the decision based

on need, value and judgment. Keep reminding yourself of this simple reality and act on it! Make the Evaluators comfortable with you, your company and product, but...

The worst selling mistakes take place when you attempt to embrace a Gatekeeper, working hard to earn their trust, hoping to win the account with an approval from Mr./Ms. Gatekeeper!

The reason we often fall into this trap is that Gatekeepers always have time to learn more, and ask for more information. They are easy to access! We, by our very nature as salespeople, feel good about having found someone who is both accessible and interested.

The problem is they do not make the decision to buy products and services. They cannot say YES or NO and sustain it! At best, they can recommend to a Recommender.

Ask yourself one additional question. What happens if I devote all my selling time and effort to Gatekeepers, and my competition sells to the Cs, Executive Buyers and Recommenders? Enough said; you know the answer!

Coaches

This is our second type of Evaluator. The Coach is that rare individual with an interest in helping you and your company to sell product to their employer. While Coaches can exist at any level in an account, they are most frequently Evaluators. We're going to focus our attention on Evaluators as Coaches. Who are these people and why do they want us to succeed? Some possibilities:

- They may have used your product in the past and enjoyed success.
- They may have worked with you, or your company, and are in a security zone.
- They may be personally comfortable with you.
- They may be misguided or misdirected.
- We may never know why or what need you fulfill for them.

While their needs are no different from the Gatekeepers, they are certainly more pleasant to work with. Therein lies the trap! We get lulled into our own desires for comfort, *"Sally really understands my product and its value. I can trust her to tell her boss and other decision makers about our solution. Everybody likes and respects her—we couldn't have a better advocate!"* I have heard and made those very statements, and, I have also lived to regret them!

Never turn your account responsibility over to a Coach!

Work with your Coaches, seek out their advice; but, judge for yourself whether their advice is good and should be acted upon. Manage your own sales process and remember: **Coaches do not buy product!**

Right this moment you may be thinking, *"This is interesting! Is there a way to know if I can trust my Coach?"* A couple of suggestions:

- As you work all the layers of The Selling Pyramid, pay a compliment about your Coach to another person in the company. *"I have really enjoyed working with Sally."* Watch and listen for the reaction!
- Ask your Coach to deliver something substantial. *"Can you get me a meeting with your Executive Buyer?"* Observe the results.

Several years ago, while immersed in a very competitive sales opportunity, I asked my Coach (I believed he was an Evaluator despite his protesting) to get me a series of meetings. Coach had assured me that he could prevail with our solution because he was very experienced in getting things done at his company. I asked to meet the Executive Buyer. Unfortunately, Coach had never met that person and seemed to lack a certain passion for trying. *"How about the CIO?"* Well, that didn't seem to be achievable either! Eventually, I arranged a meeting with both the Executive Buyer and the CIO and called my Coach to let him know about the meeting. His response? *"Wow, could you mention my name to the CIO, that would be really helpful to me!"* I was glad to do that for him. The best advice for embracing Coaches is to welcome their assistance, but verify their information.

How do I find the Decision Maker?

Start by developing a mindset, which demands an audience with Cs and Executive Buyers. This, alone, will dramatically increase your competitive performance. The attitude needs to be self-imposed. Knowing what you should do, and then literally doing it, is the leap you have to grow comfortable with. Strategically, you already have learned what decision makers need and the message to deliver. Remember the old saying...*Practice makes perfect!*

Finding a decision maker often requires a bit of detective work, patience and networking. When you're working a new prospect or account, I have found asking this question pays enormous dividends: *"Who will make the final decision?"* Sometimes people will tell you, *"I don't know,"* or *"It's certainly not me."* Sometimes, they'll lead you right to the door of the executive in charge. Ask yourself if this individual fits the criteria we have attached to a C or Executive Buyer? If they do...great! If not, keep looking!

The Selling Pyramid presents you with a clear competitive advantage. While competitors continue struggling with the question of who to approach for sales, pursuing the wrong audience and delivering messages that set their efforts back, you will know better. Identifying the ever-available Evaluators frees you from wasting precious time with people who ask questions but don't place orders. I'm not suggesting you should ignore Evaluators! Just don't trap yourself into asking them to make a sale for you or your business.

In a competitive business environment, telling the wrong people why they should purchase your product is counter-productive for two reasons. It diminishes your limited selling time and gives the competition a free opportunity to deal exclusively with the real decision makers. Few business people can afford to make that mistake very often.

Our next chapter explores the issue of personality traits and why they matter. All Cs and Executive Buyers are not the same. First, we'll identify the distinct personality types, and then discuss why specific personalities present unique competitive opportunities and challenges.

TEST YOUR KNOWLEDGE

1. Decision makers, who decide the outcome of competitive contests, can be described as..

- ❑ **Smart, witty and wonderful ladies and gentlemen;**
- ❑ **Difficult, deceptive and worse;**
- ❑ **All of the above;**
- ❑ **None of the above.**

2. Selling time is finite. **True/False**

3. What is the Selling Pyramid?

....

....

4. Cs have the following needs...

- ❑ **A discount from list price;**
- ❑ **The most robust product;**
- ❑ **Profits and increased market share;**
- ❑ **None of the above.**

5. The quicker you find and engage the Executive Buyer, the more time you will have for the real decision makers. **True/False**

6. Recommenders are the people who...

- ❑ **Use your product and are affected by its impact;**
- ❑ **Need to know detailed product functions/features;**
- ❑ **Need security and comfort;**
- ❑ **All of the above.**

7. There are two types of Evaluators—Gatekeepers and Coaches. **True/False**

8. Evaluators will focus on which two of the following?

- ❑ **Collecting information;**
- ❑ **The evaluation process;**
- ❑ **Introducing you to other decision makers;**
- ❑ **Promoting the product they select.**

9-10. Draw the Selling Pyramid and its incumbents.

CHAPTER 6

Personality Traits Influence Competitive Selections

THE FOUR PERSONALITY TRAITS

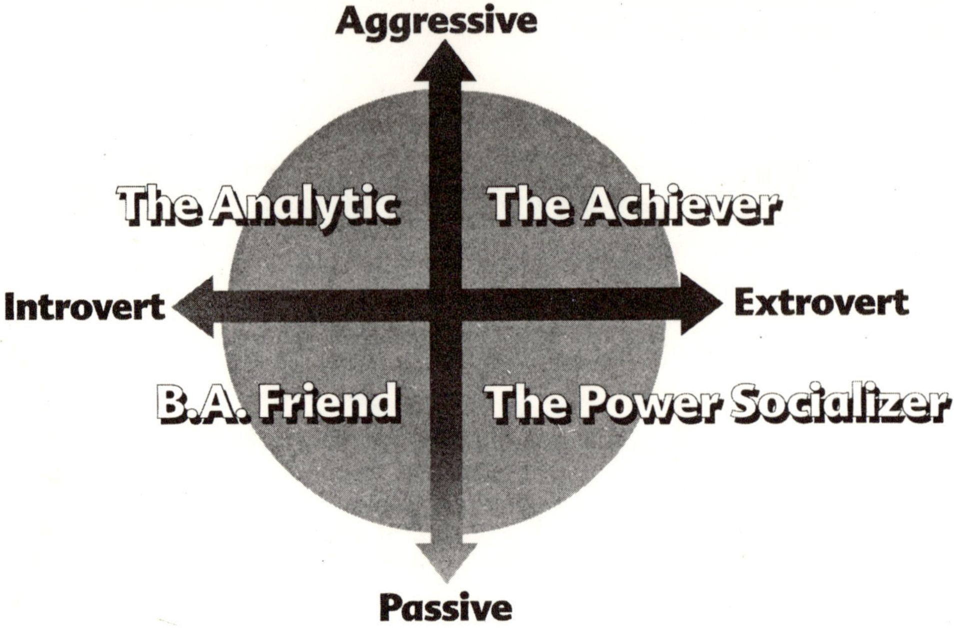

Prospects will each have their own unique personality traits. Understanding these personalities will give you invaluable insights when you attempt to persuade decision makers to choose your solution.

The Selling Pyramid identifies the needs of key decision makers. We learned what message matters most to Cs, Executive Buyers, etc. Now, the next step in ***Winning Business from Difficult Competitors*** is to identify each personality in order to communicate a message more effectively. Having the correct message is critical, but presenting it in the wrong way will diminish its power.

The matrix at the center of our discussion has two axes of behavior: *Aggressive/Passive* and *Introverted/Extroverted.* The model produces four basic personality profiles. The profiles are not the result of either scientific research or validated psychology studies. They are, in fact, the observations of a sales practitioner with a layman's interest in human behavior and significant life experience.

I have created this matrix to allow you to visualize clearly each personality profile as a blend of Aggressive/Passive behavior, as well as Extroverted/Introverted characteristics. Very few people exist as a pure

100% Analytic, Achiever, Power Socializer or B.A. Friend. Most of us are a measured blend of personality. The characteristics of our behavior can vary with time, circumstance and the situations in which we are placed. We do, however, possess one personality profile to which we return time and again.

How can I identify a personality trait?

Personal observations, research and asking others to share their experiences will help get you started. The more you know the person you're calling on and the more time you spend with them, the easier it will be to identify their personality trait. It's difficult to reach valid conclusions about people you have little or no personal interaction with. Just as first impressions are not always correct, relying on rumors or third party opinions are not reliable either.

Ask mutual friends, colleagues or business associates to share their experiences. *"I am trying to do business with...Can you share with me your impression of what he/she is like? Can you give me any advice?"* Listen, be attentive, polite and positive. Thank the other party for sharing their observations. Ask questions, but don't get drawn into making controversial remarks, insinuations, or worse yet, agreeing with any negative statements. Assume the person you are asking about will eventually find out about your inquiry and the conversation itself.

You may want to mention to your prospect you had a conversation with a mutual acquaintance. I related such a conversation to a prospect. He inquired, *"Did she say anything nice about me?"* I assured him she had, in fact, been very complimentary. *"Did she tell you she's my ex-wife?"* In truth, she had not...but I was thankful I had been 100% positive during my discussions about her former husband. Laughing, he said, *"I think I'll call and tell her you were too polite to give her up!"*

Some people will be easier than others to understand or connect with. You may have second impressions about particular personalities. Don't rush to judgment! If getting comfortable with a person comes quickly or gradually—that's okay. The answer rarely needs to be immediate.

When you call on decision makers, you gain the advantage of observing them in meetings, watching them react with staff, and perhaps interacting with other people from your own company. The impressions will help you decipher their personality profile. I should also add that calling on decision makers will provide you with benefits well beyond the scope of our present discussion points. I have learned from experience that the image people project to a particular audience is not always accurate. I can recall watching executives, who were polite and courteous with me, behave quite the opposite with their employees and peers.

Researching press articles, news stories and other public information sources can help you form your opinion. How are they described in these articles? Does the description seem consistent? Does it match your own impression? The more information you have, the better your knowledge base becomes.

There are countless books, college courses and educational seminars to help develop real proficiency in understanding human behavior and personalities. Read the works of several experts you find enjoyable. When you combine your own learning experiences with educational opportunities, you'll quickly expand your own knowledge and expertise. Experience is always a great teacher!

THE FOUR PERSONALITY TRAITS

The Achiever

These individuals are both aggressive and extroverted. Their natural disposition and mindset is driven by a sense of urgency. They are control oriented and are most comfortable when they are in charge.

Achievers are often goal oriented and very determined to reach challenging objectives. They can be personable, but their agenda is clear: deliver results or get out of the way! They will take risks to get what they want and can be quick to reach decisions. Their self-image is focused on both professional behavior and results. Achievers are most comfortable with people they view as fellow professionals. They'll socialize with other successful and influential people. Business associates who can assist them in getting what they want are important.

How a product or solution gets results is interesting, but not important. Details do not matter as much as results! Products that offer exceptional benefits or break the status quo are viewed as attractive.

Key Communication Actions:

- Give them straightforward and direct answers to questions.
- Be brief and time efficient.
- Listen carefully, they will often tell you exactly what they want.
- Your proposals must be well organized and logically presented.
- Fix any problems immediately.
- Give them a range of choices and alternatives to consider.
- Be certain you deliver on your commitments; they have a limited tolerance for mistakes and disappointments.

The ranks of Cs and Executive Buyers are heavily populated with Achievers. They will often choose other Achievers as the key members of their staff and management team.

Changing The Achiever's Position:
How can I best get an Achiever to change a position on my offering? The key is to offer a crisp, logical, non-emotional counter-argument supported by as many facts as possible.

- Preface the discussion with a neutral statement.
  "Thanks for giving me the opportunity to persuade you to select my product."
  "I may not be able to change your mind, but I sincerely appreciate the chance to do so!"
- Don't attempt to blame the Achiever for mistakes, errors or misunderstandings. Any blame is squarely in your court.
  "I may not have made this point clearly..."
  "I should have done a better job explaining..."
  The message—their decision makes perfect sense, as a result of the errors you have committed.
- You want the Achiever to reconsider the decision on the basis of the new factual information now being correctly communicated and presented. Reconsideration becomes a valid decision, because the Achiever may benefit.
- Keep the presentation concise and targeted with a focus on results. Long ramblings or emotional appeals will not be well received!
- The tone of your presentation should be upbeat, positive and candid. You want the Achiever to see you as a professional who is admitting and correcting a problem.
- Being a good loser will keep the door open to other opportunities. Poor losers rarely get to come back under any circumstance.

CASE STUDY
Introductory Meeting With The Achiever

The view from the 37th floor corner office was breathtaking. Abe regaled in pointing out the city's sights and landmarks. This was his space and he was in full command! Our meeting came from a referral by a current customer who told me, *"I understand our competitor is going to enter into consumer lending, you may as well have another customer in town."* My phone call to Abe resulted in the meeting this morning.

Two questions were to be answered in the next 30 minutes: could my product meet his potential needs and did I have the ability to deliver value to Abe personally? The pace of the conversation would be quick, focused and follow the plan I had carefully crafted. I knew my 30 minutes would expire right on schedule!

His reputation was punctuated with such words as intense, serious and driven. A colleague described him as being determined to run his company and having little reservation about his intentions.

I was also warned, *"He's not going to tolerate a disorganized presentation or the person who presents it!"*

"I read an article about you in Banker's Daily just yesterday, were you pleased with the story?"

Abe smiled politely, *"Just the good parts, the rest was just nonsense!"* He displayed more humor than I would have expected, *"But you didn't come here to discuss news stories, did you?"*

"No, I didn't. I'm not sure if I can help you, but if you could share with me your strategy for entering consumer banking, I may be able to offer some products to assist you. As you know, our company has significant experience and expertise in this area."

He talked and I listened. He was direct and clear about what he needed. I confirmed for him my belief his plans were ambitious but manageable.

"Your plan to enter the consumer lending business is very similar to several customers we have recently worked with. Let me give you the condensed version of how we assisted both of them..." I had his full attention.

"Abe...the bottom line is this product will grow revenue by allowing you to offer a portfolio of new customer services and it is engineered to keep operating expenses to a minimum. The range of products you can provide your market is far more flexible and robust

than your competition will allow."

He asked about a customer who was a direct competitor of his.

"They use our product for essentially the same portfolio of lending products you're planning. I can't disclose the details of how or what specifically without securing their approval...we have to respect our customers wishes for limited confidentiality."

His impatience was obvious. *"Can you get approval for a discussion with them? How long will that take?"*

"Abe, I can call David Wilson this afternoon. Whether he will agree to share his experience with you is up to him; but, David, like you, is the Chief Operating Officer. I have to respect any commitments we have made to him. I will get you several other reference accounts under any circumstances."

"This is very, very good...excellent!" His excitement was real.

"I can't tell you how important this new market is to this bank and to me, personally! A success at our institution would be valuable to you. I can use my connections to introduce your company to other executives who'll need the same products."

Time was running out. *"Abe, it appears to me we have discussed a number of your needs...I believe a second more detailed discussion is in order. The agenda for the meeting should include..."*

"I agree, but I want additional information about... I will want to hear from you tomorrow morning with the results of your telephone call. I also need you to meet my staff." He was already comfortably exercising his, 'I'm in charge' prerogative.

As I shook his hand to leave, he made one last comment.

"I run a professional organization, which means I only deal with real professionals, whether they work for me, with me or sell to me. I'm looking forward to working with you...and finding out how good of a salesperson you prove to be!"

B.A. Friend

Friendship, cooperation and job security are at the core of this personality. The incumbents have a genuinely engaging and friendly demeanor. They are respectful of authority but will resist any changes to the status quo, especially if those changes adversely impact friends and colleagues. Their work groups are often viewed as family. A stable company and structured organization are important.

Their friendship needs to be cultivated. Products that change the work environment must be seen as both non-threatening and having minimal risk. Their comfort zone is very much focused on keeping things the way they currently function. The responsibility for getting the fundamental operating tasks of the business accomplished frequently falls squarely in their domain.

Key Communication Actions:

- They will place significant value on conducting business with friends. In fact, they're reluctant to purchase important products from anyone who is not considered a friend.
- A relationship, built with mutual respect and trust, opens the door to future business opportunities.
- Be patient and non-threatening.
- Offer personal commitments and keep them.
- Avoid any argumentative behavior or circumstances; they value co-operation, not confrontation.
- Do not pressure them to make decisions.

B.A. Friends are most prevalent in the role of Recommenders. They are rarely encountered as Cs or Executive Buyers. The ranks of Evaluator-Coaches are populated with this personality type.

Changing B.A. Friend's Position:
Appeal to the decision maker as a friend and remind him/her of the risks involved with his/her choice. *"I have to tell, you as a friend, this decision is very risky!"*

- Explain why your offering is a better choice.
- Extend your personal commitment to their past, present and future success.
- Ask them to share, as a friend, why they have come to believe your proposal must be rejected.
- Keep the discussion friendly and non-threatening.

- *"Our friendship is too important to jeopardize."*
- Offer a compromise. *"This is a good discussion, now I realize how important an extended warranty is to you! Suppose I was able to..."*

CASE STUDY
Asking For B.A. Friend's Business

The conference room was well worn as were the folding chairs and table. Department managers had basement offices, which were much too small for any meetings...much different than life on the 37th floor.

Anne had assembled her team for yet another session to review the workflow for the new lending platform. The room was packed; obviously, a conscientious effort to include everyone whose job would be affected by this project.

Anne was clearly in charge, her demeanor was polite, friendly and concerned. The group dynamics reminded me of a large extended family gathering for an important decision. Every supervisor and employee brought their list of questions and concerns.

Eileen Rivers was our Sales Support representative and doubled occasionally as a Product Installation Manager. It was her job to answer every product-related question and dispense advice about the use of the proposed system. No one ever doubted her expertise for even a minute. Her enthusiasm was genuine and contagious. As a former teacher, Eileen answered each question and responded to each concern, real or imagined, the blackboards were full of diagrams and notes. After the meeting, I took Anne and Eileen to dinner for a wrap-up discussion.

"Anne are there any questions we have remaining or any open issues? We want to be sure you're comfortable we can do just what we have promised...without any surprises!"

She seemed flustered, *"This is a bit overwhelming. We're being asked to do something we have little knowledge or experience with. I want to be sure my people are not asked to do the impossible, or worse yet, blamed if something goes wrong!"* She rolled her eyes and confided, *"Abe, in case you don't know, doesn't deal well with failure!"*

"Anne, I don't know Abe as well as you do, but I do understand he expects results first and foremost. We're also at a point where we need your recommendation for the purchase of our product. Are you ready to do that?"

Her frown was almost painful. *"It's not a simple decision. I far prefer doing business with you and Eileen than your competitor. I'm just struggling with any decision."*

We ate in silence until I suggested:

"Anne, let's try this, just to see if we can get you comfortable with working with us. Suppose, Eileen spent the next 3 months working in your department helping you every day get the process started, with the option for a second three months if you personally feel you need extra assistance? Eileen would have to clear her calendar, and Abe will have to foot some extra expenses. I don't normally offer this service, but I want you to know we are personally committed to helping you through this project!"

Her face lit up as if it were Christmas morning. *"I consider Eileen a true friend—my employees and I would accept that arrangement in a heartbeat! Would you really do that for me?"*

"Make this part of your recommendation, and I promise you I will figure out how to get this deal done!"

Anne's recommendation was celebrated!

The Analytic

Aggressive, but introverted, describe the hallmarks of this personality type. The details matter to Analytics, they will act only when they are comfortable with the facts of any proposed change.

Change for the sake of change is an anathema. The saying, *"Don't fix it if it's not broke!"* and *"Show me!"* are excellent summations of the mindset they bring to business and life. They cannot be persuaded to act on a whim; and when they do act, they require the security of detailed studies. Making safe decisions are a hallmark of this personality.

They are often criticized for not being visionary or big-picture oriented.

Key Communication Actions:

- Your presentations must be orderly, logical and supported by detailed facts. Big-picture, vague statements or claims will not be well received.
- References...References!

- Expect that all your claims will be verified.
- The organization and preciseness of managing the sales process is very important. A disorganized sales performance will create a serious obstacle to your proposal being accepted.
- Low risk and safety are key product features for this audience.
- Product warranties and service guarantees should be presented and reviewed in detail.
- Patience is critical, both in building a relationship and finalizing the terms of a business transaction.

Analytics can be found in every role in business organizations. They're heavily represented in financial assignments, but it's a mistake to fail to appreciate the broad reach of this personality. The executive suite, Cs and Executive Buyers are heavily populated with Analytics. The ranks of entrepreneurs also include a significant number.

Changing The Analytic's Position:
You can't appeal to friendship or attempt to debate obscure issues! You need to find out what they specifically view as your deficiency, and then present the facts to prove they have missed the point. Getting a decision factually correct is very important to this personality.

- It's paramount to get specific issues on the table. Probing and questioning are essential parts of any conversation with Analytics. Remember, these are detail-oriented people. You can't change their minds without the benefit of those same details.
- Becoming emotional with Analytics will not succeed. Keep your conversations and presentations orderly, polite and to the point.
- If you can show an Analytic they misunderstood a detail, regardless of whose fault it was, or missed a key point of information, they can and will reverse their position.
- The problem for Analytics is in the 'grey' areas. They will struggle with understanding and interpreting conflicting facts. Be very consistent in your message and arguments.
- Safety and security are important. Asking Analytics to change, or take risk, has to be buttressed with an appeal that recognizes the need to manage risk to acceptable levels. *"I know my proposal has an element of risk associated with it. Here's how we propose to limit and manage your risk..."*

CASE STUDY
Competing For The Analytic's Business

Ed Smart peered over his glasses, *"I'm paying for 90 days of support, a hotel, rental car and meals? Why would I do this? No one else is asking for this kind of money! We may be a bank...but we're not Fort Knox! You do understand nothing gets done without my approval?"*

I knew this would be the first of several conversations the CFO and I were about to have. Abe himself had warned me that no detail was too small for Ed. Several other officers expressed the belief, *"Ed is not sold on consumer banking as either a good strategy or investment."*

"Before we get sidetracked about the costs included in our proposal, Ed, perhaps we should talk about our experience in consumer banking and some of the current customers."

Ed seemed to reset his focus and commented, *"Good idea—let's start at the beginning and plow through this step-by-step. I really want to hear about other banker's experiences."*

"With our product or with consumer banking?" I asked.

"Both," was his reply.

"Ed, I have two questions. Are you willing to visit several reference accounts to ask your questions directly? And, will you put together a list of issues and specific questions for our visits?"

He seemed interested, *"Set the meetings up...you will have the questions in 48 hours!"*

We spent four long days visiting accounts. He asked his questions and got both advice and answers. Ed filled a good-sized pad with his carefully constructed notes. He often asked me, *"Did I hear this right?" "Is this note I made correct?"* Around Day 3, the skepticism gave way and the questions began to focus on the 'how' not 'if' we do this.

"Tom, we have to really discuss support and how you intend to guarantee we're successful. Can you arrange for me to meet Eileen? Who else will be assigned to our account? What will the service agreement include? What's your plan for the next steps?"

Questions seeking details!

"Ed, are you ready to recommend the purchase of our product to Abe?"

"I am comfortable you are TNBT and soon will be the Gold Standard in this market, and selecting a market leader is very important to me, but we still have open issues to resolve."

"Okay Ed, let's create a list of issues to be resolved. When we agree to terms for those items, I can expect your recommendation... Correct?"

"Yes!" Ed confirmed.

"Ed, the question of risk is your decision. You can eliminate the cost for Eileen's on-site assistance, which means the bank accepts responsibility for most installation tasks. I doubt the costs will go away, just remember this expense item will amount to less than 2% of your budgeted project costs."

The first issue had now become the last issue! A long moment later...Ed reached his decision.

"I don't want the risk! Expenses will need to be covered under our standard travel policy. I will personally arrange for a corporate apartment, use of a bank automobile and our standard per-diem living allowance. If this is acceptable, you have my recommendation."

The Power Socializer

Acceptance and social inclusion are paramount to this personality type; just as crucial is being popular with colleagues and business associates. They want to be seen in a favorable light and will work hard to reach this status.

Details are not of much interest, but big-picture issues, or popular causes are highly valued. Being recognized for their contributions is a front and center agenda item.

The enjoyment of inclusion and acceptance can be so powerful that getting a project completed becomes secondary. Motivating a Power Socializer to reach a decision requires both patience and an incentive. They can struggle with details and often need assistance in this area.

Key Communication Actions:

- Build a relationship and camaraderie through social activities and events. Having fun is important.
- Ask for their input and opinions when you prepare a proposal.
- Introduce them to your reference accounts, so they feel included.
- Focus on the benefits of the Big Picture.
- Give them a reason to act on your proposal.
- Disagreements or criticism should never be allowed to become a personal affront.

Power Socializers can be found throughout The Selling Pyramid. They frequent assignments with responsibility for customers, prospects and other external stakeholder audiences.

Changing The Power Socializer's Position:
Criticize the decision, not the person making it, and be very careful to preserve the relationship. Why? It's about acceptance and inclusion!
Don't argue details, appeal to the bigger issues and relationships.
"We are a high-profile player in our market—our competitor isn't. We really want you to be a partner in the exciting things we have planned for this product. You don't want to miss the important publicity and recognition we can jointly enjoy!"
Stress that the decision is about more than just a single product or its features. The decision is about being part of a group, which can change, impact or affect marketplaces, industries or business in general.

CASE STUDY
Competing For The Power Socializer's Business

Abe left a voice message, *"I've just hired a new VP of Retail Banking, his name is Don Kelly. He's still working in New York. Call him and get his blessing on your proposal."*

My telephone call to Don was warmly received. *"Abe said I would enjoy working with you. Why don't we meet at my club for lunch tomorrow? If you get there before me, just have the maitre d' seat you at my usual table."*

I felt as if I had known Don for years! We chatted at lunch about his career in banking, his kids, my kids, colleges and baseball. Don exclaimed, "A baseball fan...let's take in a game this evening! The bank has box seats. I'll make a quick call, get the tickets, and meet you at the stadium at 6 pm!"

I told Don about the history of our company and its client base—in particular, the high-profile executives we had as loyal customers. Don knew many of these same people from his work on various committees and industry taskforces. Then I took him through our recommendations from both Ed and Anne.

"You need to be comfortable with the proposal because you will

become the executive user of the product. The proposal will allow the bank to grow its revenue with a portfolio of new customer services and keep the operating expenses to a minimum." Don seemed to be completely at ease with the decision his new colleagues had already reached. It was clear being seen as a team player was important. I decided to take one additional step.

"Don, our chairman will be in New York next week for a series of meetings, and on Friday he is going to fly west to meet Abe. Would you be available for a lunch or dinner meeting earlier in the week?" He graciously accepted the offer and we agreed I would work out the details.

The Chairman had two assignments: Be certain Don knew we valued the opportunity to have him as a customer, and invite him to join our exclusive user's group, the Chairman's Advisory Circle. Needless to say, only customers belong to this group!

Our dinner meeting was a success. Don was at his jovial charming best and very gracious. Unfortunately, he was also in no hurry to make any recommendations. *"I will need several months to get settled in my new assignment. I'm sure your solution is the best choice, but I'll need to consult with my colleagues and staff. Perhaps, I could participate in the Advisory Circle on an interim basis, until we officially become a customer?"*

"Don, the council is strictly for customers and the offer is on the table until month end. I wish I could extend it, but the chairman also has another candidate for the open seat. How can I help you get the recommendation finalized?"

"Tom, can't you buy me more time?" Don looked frustrated and uncomfortable. *"I really want to be part of this council."*

"Don, suppose I speak with Abe, tell him you want to be part of the council, but are concerned about the timing of your decision. Can I tell him I have your informal recommendation?"

"Sure, just make it clear I'm fully behind the conclusion Anne and Ed reached, but I need to finish some other commitments before I can fully focus on this project."

Abe glared across the table at me and slowly shook his head. *"Informal? Interesting! So now you and I can get down to striking a deal I am happy with..."*

The competitive arena is not a level playing field.

The personality traits of the people who select the winning vendors give some contestants a decided advantage. This knowledge presents you the opportunity to play to an advantage or to work around a challenge.

The Achiever Personality

Driven by the need to succeed, they rationalize that reaching their goals and going beyond the ordinary requires taking risks. The risks will be offset by the achievement of extraordinary gains. Finding products and companies that offer benefits that go beyond the status quo is second nature. Delivering high returns satisfies the need to excel and advance a career or business. Unless they are pre-occupied or view a particular purchase as mundane, the desire to break barriers will govern.

The Achiever Personality will seek out:

- The Next Big Thing
- Mystics
- Brand New

Each of these competitive types offers the leap forward in profit, revenue growth, and expense reduction so valued by the incumbent personality.

Some years ago, as a star salesperson for a Gold Standard company, I began to notice a fascinating phenomenon. New competitors began to enter our marketplace with an interesting 'story'. I use the word story because, in most cases, the product they offered was just that–a tale! The best this group could claim was perhaps several reference accounts; others had little more than presentation slides to represent a product.

They began to win business! I clearly remember several long airplane rides wondering how I could lose to a product that was questionably real. The fog began to lift as I discovered that my competitors were targeting accounts with **Achiever** decision makers and playing to their desire for extraordinary returns on invested capital. The aggressive personalities were saying loud and clear, I will take risks to get extraordinary results. In fact, the more people that committed to this risk scenario, the more acceptable and fashionable it became. Other Achievers began to say, *"I couldn't afford to be left behind, regardless of the risk!"*

Gold Standard became the solution when the product claims became so preposterous that even the Achiever personalities began to back away.

The Achiever Personality will avoid:

- Mainstream
- Peripherals
- Bottom Feeders

Achiever has several problems with this group of competitors. They're viewed as, at best, status quo and, at worst, they lack the professional standing and appeal to satisfy basic ego demands. To prevail with this personality type, Mainstream, Peripheral or Bottom Feeder must have an extraordinary proposal. The offer most attractive is a significant pricing or business term concession. Achiever must be able to rationalize that this was such a great deal he could not refuse the offer!

The Compromise Solution:
Gold Standard will be the compromise solution if claims are too ridiculous and unsubstantiated. The lack of a credible Mystic, The Next Big Thing, or Brand New contestant will result in Gold Standard's selection. It's a mistake to view the selection as anything other than temporary and convenient. Unless Gold Standard introduces a break-through product or service, however, they are flirting with elimination.

The Analytic Personality

The two characteristics at the forefront of this personality are details and safe decision-making. Every piece of your proposal will be carefully examined and vetted. Expect requests for any missing information and lots of clarification questions. Before the status quo can be changed, the Analytic will need to be comfortable with you, your company and the product. A patient approach to building a relationship will be well received. Evolutionary change is preferred to revolutionary shifts, and references are paramount. I can assure you the references will be carefully checked! Analytics can be aggressive and tough negotiators.

The Analytic Personality will seek out:

- Gold Standard
- Mainstream

The desire to make safe decisions, that bring evolutionary changes to the status quo, plays to the strength of Gold Standard and Mainstream businesses. Analytics are loyal customers and can be difficult to take from an incumbent vendor. Why? Change equates to risk; and risk is something to be avoided.

The Analytic Personality will avoid:

- Mystics
- Peripherals
- Bottom Feeders
- Brand New

Each of these competitive profiles has risk inherent in either their business or product offering. References are a problem for Mystics and Brand New.

The Compromise Solution:
When Gold Standard or Mainstream fails in its selling efforts or product offering, The Next Big Thing will become the fall back. The more references and customers that exist, the better Analytics will feel about selecting the compromise solution. The challenge for TNBT is to demonstrate that they are not Mystics and the risk of selection is minimal.

B.A. Friend Personality

Friendships, security, and support for the status quo. They need to see any change as evolutionary and it must have a minimal impact on the friendships that support their work groups. Competitors who have established a friendship will be given every consideration, despite not fitting the ideal profile. The longer the friendship, the stronger will be the desire to continue the relationship. They are not quite as unpredictable as Power Socializers, but the bonds of friendship are strong.

B.A. Friend Personality will seek out:

- Gold Standard
- Mainstream

Secure, well-known and pro-status quo will always have the upper hand. If either of these competitive types is the incumbent vendor, they will be difficult to dislodge.

B.A. Friend Personality will avoid:

- Mystics
- Peripherals
- Bottom Feeders
- Brand New

Conversely, any vendor associated with risk, or an evolutionary change proponent, will always be disadvantaged. However, an established friendship can impact B.A. Friend and disrupt the normal behavior pattern. For example, a Bottom Feeder who has a long standing friendship and an established vendor record can become a competitive force. Brand New represented by a familiar owner or salesperson can also become a viable choice.

The Compromise Solution:
A momentum player like The Next Big Thing will be embraced if Gold Standard or Mainstream cannot meet the prescribed product or business needs. Momentum will be viewed as an acceptable risk, especially if their product is positioned as an evolutionary business step and a diligent attempt is made to build a new friendship.

The Power Socializer Personality

The wild card of personalities! The need for acceptance and social inclusion can ultimately lead Power Socializers to embrace any of the competitive profiles. They can be very active participants in social causes and fashionable organizations, these events and social gatherings allow them to build a long list of friends and acquaintances. The fact that they enjoy the opportunity to talk with people makes them accessible to most competitors. Since details are not a priority, they are open to being persuaded and courted by business people from the full range of competitors.

The Power Socializer Personality will seek out:

- Gold Standard, TNBT, Mainstream, Mystics, Peripherals, Brand New and Bottom Feeders.
- The competitor who is best able to make them feel accepted, appreciated and included. Entertainment and socializing are important parts of their on-going business life.
- Those who ask for their advice and consent.
- A prestigious or socially connected company.
- A salesperson that demonstrates they can get a commitment without confrontational behavior. Personal appeals are often most effective, *"I personally need your business this month, can you help me out?"*

The Power Socializer is not naturally detail-oriented. They will often have a partner, or business associate that is responsible for the details. The personality of this individual can be critical. They will select from competitors based on the advice of this advisor, who may well be an Achiever or

Analytic with their own pre-dispositions. Watch for this person! Often the advisor will deliver any bad news for the Power Socializer, who will be more sensitive to preserving relationships than other personality types.

Business people should focus on creating and sustaining long-term relationships with Power Socializers. Entertaining this personality is an important part of creating and supporting interaction and friendships.

The Power Socializer Personality will avoid:

- Competitors with little interest in building personal relationships.
- Bottom Feeders in particular, or others with reputations that conflict with popular social issues. Falling into disfavor with colleagues or being cited by business associates for embracing an unpopular vendor is not acceptable.
- People who push for or demand decisions!

Losing an order, while disappointing, should be viewed as a temporary set-back that can be corrected in the next decision cycle. Power Socializers have lots of friends; therefore, it may take patience before you are finally selected as a business partner. Anything even approaching confrontational behavior, as the result of a lost proposal, will accomplish very little. Over the longer term, your best strategy may be to work the relationship and just wait your turn!

The Compromise Solution:
Unfortunately, not making a timely decision is often The Power Socializer's way of escaping from conflicting proposals and overwhelming details.

Each of these four personality traits brings to the evaluation process an initial predisposition or mindset. Successful competitors understand how to work with each persona to present their solution in the most favorable way possible–reinforcing initial judgments when appropriate, and persuading ever present skeptics where necessary!

Influence gravitates to senior positions.

Two examples: An Achiever holding the position of Chief or Executive Buyer is far more important to The Next Big Thing than having an Achiever in the position of Evaluator. Conversely, Analytic as the Executive Buyer will make Gold Standard a favorite in a competitive sale. The same personality as a Coach will not provide as much competitive influence.

The Cs and Executive Buyers personally decide, give support to or exercise veto power over most business commitments. They'll either support or oppose the selection of a specific competitor. Regardless of an initial favorable or unfavorable position, you must interact with these decision makers.

Knowing who will make the final decision and learning their personality profile, allows you to engage in a dialog to reinforce your competitive strengths and to argue credibly against disqualification.

The strategy and organizational culture of a business is greatly influenced by its executive team. In fact, many companies are an extension of their owner's or executive manager's personality profiles. The better you understand what matters to the top executives or owners, and why it's important, the quicker you can focus your competitive efforts.

Don't allow yourself to be the competitor who is *missing in action!* In other words, don't be the only competitor that doesn't meet with the prospect's top executives! Your absence will be noted and not in a particularly favorable way.

I have always competed by embracing this theory: Until told differently, always assume the top decision makers want to meet you! They alone have the ability to refuse this meeting, but it's your responsibility to ask.

What if I know, or have reason to believe, a specific person will oppose my solution? Should I avoid this person? Work around them?

No! Always meet with people who are opposed to your proposal!
Why?

- To fully understand their objections. Suppose they are mistaken about an important fact or simply missed a critical concept. You don't want to lose an important prospect over a misunderstanding. That's truly a lose-lose scenario.
- You want the opportunity to persuade them your solution is both appropriate and valuable to their business. The attempt to persuade is not always destined to succeed. It's also not doomed to 100% guaranteed failure! Reaching an agreement to disagree or securing a partial acknowledgement of your value is often a victory.

Analytics who are Recommenders may still prefer Gold Standard and be reluctant to embrace Mystics. An Achiever may be more favorable to The Next Big Thing than a Bottom Feeder. Persuading them to carefully consider your proposal, at least, is far better than leaving their objections unaddressed.

I have watched countless supporters of the competition change their position or moderate their objections: B.A. Friends who decide they can trust, Power Socializers who enjoyed your company, Analytics who discovered new facts, and Achievers who realize you can deliver value. They may agree to consent to the wisdom of your supporters, decide to stay out of the decision process or choose to embrace your proposal. None of which can occur until you undertake deliberate action!

A common competitive error is to avoid people who either object directly to your offering or are suspect. My point is, they exist in almost every opportunity and need to be engaged and persuaded.

The importance of appealing to the top decision makers should not exclude you from earning the respect, support and approval of Recommenders and Evaluators. It pays dividends to invest the time and effort to build working relationships.

Successful businesspeople understand they need to win the support or at least minimize the points of resistance across the complete Selling Pyramid. Knowing how to work with each personality profile will help you to do just that!

The People Who Influence Competitive Choices builds on Part I and introduces you to a second stage of competitive reality and complexity. The businessmen and women who decide competitive contests are unique and often have their own preferences! Each of the four personalities will instinctively seek out specific competitors to get the solution they believe best meets their needs.

The more senior the position a person holds in The Selling Pyramid, the greater the influence he or she can exert on the final competitive results. When you understand the needs and personalities of the people who make the decisions to purchase, and how best to influence their instinctive choices, you have an enormous competitive advantage.

Winning new customers, securing new orders, and getting repeat business from existing accounts is an ongoing competitive process. The complexity may seem overwhelming at first glance! But, as you gain experience in the competitive arena—the concepts, logic and benefits of our approach will become very clear.

Just remember that competing successfully for business bestows great rewards...rewards that make the challenge worthwhile!

TEST YOUR KNOWLEDGE

1. List the four identified personality traits of prospects.

....

....

2. Achievers can be both aggressive and extroverted. True/False

3. When you communicate with an Achiever...

- ❑ Take your time...slow and steady!
- ❑ Give them only one choice.
- ❑ Give them straightforward answers to questions
- ❑ Be sure written proposals are artistic and polished.

4. Analytics are all about friendship and money. True/False

5. When you communicate with.. be sure to:

- ❑ Build a friendly relationship.
- ❑ Be patient and non-threatening.
- ❑ Don't pressure them to make decisions.
- ❑ Offer personal commitments.

6. Details matter to.., they will act only when they are comfortable with the facts of any proposed change.

7. Understanding the personality traits of the people who select the winning vendors presents an opportunity to play to an advantage or work around a challenge. True/False

8. The Achiever personality will seek out Mainstream, Peripheral and Bottom Feeder competitors. True/False

9. Analytics are most comfortable doing business with which two of the following...

- ❑ Mystics
- ❑ Gold Standard
- ❑ Brand New
- ❑ Mainstream

10. The more senior the positions specific personalities occupy in The Selling Pyramid, the greater their competitive influence. True/False

WINNING BUSINESS

CHAPTER 7

Competing Efficiently

Winning Business is not a one-time event. You need to prevail consistently over your competitors to prosper. I want you to discard one very common and dangerous piece of business folklore...

> **I will compete anytime, anywhere,**
> **with anyone, for any opportunity!**

Competing efficiently is built on two foundational concepts:

- Managing your selling time and capital.
- Winning a high percentage of the contests you enter.

Every business and its employees have at their disposal limited amounts of selling time. Every minute you choose to spend with a particular prospect...is time you can't recover. Many businesses only have access to their prospects for 40 to 50 hours each week. In some cases, the available hours may be even fewer!

If you spend too much time with prospects who can't or won't purchase your product, you limit your success and deprive yourself of time that could have been spent with prospects who want to buy your product. If you waste your selling time performing unproductive and unnecessary administrative tasks or other time consuming trivia, you end up with the same problem. Managing your selling time is a challenge and opportunity. Savvy businesspeople jealously guard the use of their selling time because it is a limited resource. The same logic applies to the use of capital.

The corollary to this reality is that no one will prevail in 100% of the competitive opportunities they undertake. The cost of competing for business is real and discernable. Spending your limited selling time competing against those you prevail over 10% of the time is a mistake. Not many businesses can succeed in an environment where they lose 90% of the opportunities they pursue. This is where the false notion—*any contest you can participate in is worth pursuing*—is truly exposed as myth.

Using your time to compete with those you beat in 70% of your contests is more productive. Smart business people understand that using finite time and capital wisely requires deciding when to compete for business and when to walk away! How do you make this decision? Is it dangerous to abandon a potential opportunity? Chapter 3 revealed the Seven Competitors with the strengths and weaknesses of each profile. We have also reviewed the best and worst of competitive match-ups. The value of this material is to allow you to determine which particular competitors and personalities best suit your needs for securing new business. For example, your company may always beat Gold Standard when the decision maker at the prospect account is an Achiever. Perhaps you prevail over Mystics when Analytics are in charge, but rarely overcome The Next Big Thing. This knowledge allows you to select the opportunities where you *should* invest selling time and resources—the high-probability wins you can take to the proverbial bank!

Those match-ups that favor a particular competitor may be tempting to pursue. After all, very few of us want to back away from a challenge. Losing an opportunity by not competing seems wasteful, even difficult to do! In a perfect world with unlimited resources and capital, you might decide never to walk away. Think of the challenge as a poker hand—would you continue to play a bad hand? Would you do this again and again, risking hundreds or thousands of dollars, only to predictably finish out of the money?

> **Niche your business around high-probability competitive contests that you win again and again. When you have exhausted one, find another that produces high-probability victories. Build your business on these opportunistic matches.**

Let the competitors that you do not prevail against win their deals at another's expense! Use your time prospecting for and qualifying high-probability prospects and competitive matches.

I can recall being derided by a competitor who crowed he had not seen us in many large deals recently. The insinuation was that we had no appetite to compete with his company. He was absolutely correct! We had built a great business selling to accounts that were far too small and cost-conscious to purchase the high-end product he sold. In our collective wisdom, he was not a competitor! We viewed his company as the dominant player in a market we did not serve.

When he and his colleagues wandered into our niche, we quickly disposed of them. What they resented was that we were also too smart to play on their home turf. I am sure they would have relished a punching bag they could safely overcome.

Despite their success with large accounts, they ended up as an acquisition. The market had too few large participants to support a high-end high-cost vendor. We had a large and growing base of small businesses that proliferated in this particular marketplace. We entered the upscale market only after we acquired our boisterous friend and changed the economics of their business!

High-probability prospects provide positive leverage of your time and capital!

Asking a prospect these questions can help to evaluate the potential cost of competing.

- Which other vendors are you considering?
- How do you intend to reach a decision?
- When will the decision be made?
- Are the budget and the funding in place?

Which other vendors are you considering?
Early in your prospecting and qualifying activities, you will want to ask this question. The answer you receive is important! Is the prospect looking at the competitors you always defeat? If they are, this is a contest you want to focus your time and energy winning.

Are they focusing on a different mix of contestants? When this happens, the question you need answered is twofold: Who are these businesses? and...How does the purchaser see my company fitting into this group? The most important challenge to address is the question of need. Have you misunderstood the prospect's need or have they misunderstood your product's value? Here's a common experience:

"I don't recognize any of the companies you have listed as my competitors for your business. I just want to be sure I understand what you need, and how we can best fulfill those requirements."

"Well, it's not likely you can meet our needs. Actually, you're a long shot on our list of potential solutions. We have a policy of always trying to purchase from existing vendors even if we have to stretch to make it work."

"You do realize I am not a current vendor?"

"Yes, but someone suggested you were possibly worth considering."

"Would it matter if we elected not to participate in this specific contest, because the fit doesn't seem to work well?"

"No, I never really considered you a real option."

"I really would like the opportunity to have you as a customer. Let me quickly take you through our product line, so we can both see how we could possibly assist you in the future!"

Sometimes, purchasers justify the selection of specific product by examining several competing offerings, which they know will not meet their needs.

"I really don't compete with Galactic Services. They serve manufacturers whose needs are far more complex and volume-driven than the solution we offer. Do you feel Galactic best suits your requirements?"

"We know Galactic has the only product to meet our needs, but we have to show we compared them to an alternative! Can't you give us a day next week to finish this evaluation?"

Requests for Proposals (RFPs) are an outstanding example of a purchaser shopping for information. The requests are often blindly sent to countless vendors who may bid a potential solution. Immeasurable hours of work and expense are often devoted to creating responses, only to be met with a simple rejection or no answer at all!

What suspects deem as good for their business may not be valuable for you. Remember, qualifying a prospect is a two-way street!

Suppose no one will tell you who the competition is? Prospects who refuse to reveal your competitor are either acting on a genuine belief the information is confidential or are hiding an agenda. As you work The Selling Pyramid, keep asking the question. My experience has been you will discover that pertinent information sooner or later.

Legitimate prospects engaged in honest competitive evaluations have no long-term interest in keeping the list of choices secret, however, they may withhold the list early in the qualification process to avoid premature discussions about adversarial strengths and weaknesses or attempts at negative selling.

When you do encounter a prospect that steadfastly refuses to discuss the competitor issue, have the following discussion with the account's Executive Buyer:

"I really want the opportunity to win your business. I'm willing to make a substantial investment of my time and resources to work with your company. Unfortunately, it's very difficult to do a professional job of competing for your order if I have no idea of the alternatives you are considering."

Executive Buyers will fully understand your position. The insistence on secrecy usually stems from Evaluators attempting to control the selling process.

Get comfortable discovering if the product you offer is a good fit for the prospect account, and if they profile as a good potential investment of your selling time and capital. One of the quickest ways to do this is to find out who's the competition! Great opportunities are punctuated by facing competitors you know and overcome each and every business day.

How do you intend to reach a decision?
This question is a calculated attempt to understand the ground rules of the competition. It will also tell you if the plan to purchase has been well thought-out. The better the purchaser's plan, the more likely it will be acted on—and finalized with the placement of an order.

Understanding the ground rules is important because you will discover not only the criteria the decision will be based upon, but also the anticipated number of meetings, presentations, and committee approvals. Incidentally, your corollary questions should include: Who will make the decision? Who will own the project? The answers and requirements may impact the time and expense needed to win the contest.

Look for provisions you cannot or will not accommodate. A request for a very specific category of reference accounts may present a problem. What if the winning vendor must post a liability bond, or use the purchaser's contractual agreements? Must your proposal include pricing governed by a most favored nation's clause? The sooner you understand and evaluate the contest rules, the quicker you can determine if the contest works for your business.

You want to avoid opportunities where the purchaser's rules prohibit you from winning, or deals that are simply too costly to engage. *"I can't afford to spend that much time and expense trying to win a $5,000 sale!"* ... *"I'm not going to sign a 200-page contract for a $2,500 order."* The time to resolve any of these challenges is before you invest in the contest, not after you have spent countless resources.

Early in my sales career, I inherited a prospect for which our company had done seven presentations—all on the same product! Each presentation represented several thousand dollars of real expense and manpower! It was always followed by an excuse, typically centered on the temporary postponement of the project. We weren't the only vendor doing these presentations. When I received the request for presentation number eight, here is how the conversation unfolded:

"We have already presented seven times, correct?"
"Yes."
"What do you expect to learn from the eighth presentation?"
"We're not sure...but we're still shopping."
"Shopping for what?"
"Information!"
"I can provide information without doing formal presentations, which are very expensive to perform."

"No, we like presentations."

"Okay. But, we only do seven presentations for any prospect at no charge. The eighth, and each event beyond, requires a fee of $5,000."

"I can't pay for a presentation! I don't have any budget for the project or the authority to authorize that kind of money!"

"Well, who does?"

There was no answer. Just silence! The only thing worse than spending $35,000 to conclude a $25,000 sale–is to spend $40,000!

When a prospect does not know how they intend to reach a decision, you're in double jeopardy. They can easily change their collective minds at any time or alter the rules in a way you can't accommodate. Some business people believe they can counsel the prospect through this challenge and set the stage for their own success by controlling the evaluation process. Personally, I've seen a lot of time and effort wasted by trying to offer free consultations rather than a business proposal.

I view prospective opportunities that are uncertain about reaching a decision as high-risk investments. A mentor used to say, *"Interesting! When you decide how you want to proceed, give me a call, I would love the chance to pick up our conversation!"*

When will the decision be made?

Winning business is only valuable if an order is placed! Being told you are the winning vendor, *"but we can't purchase,"* is not a profitable outcome.

Smart business people realize a number of purchase decisions will never be brought to completion. Unanticipated events have a way of overtaking good intentions and the best of plans. Asking and re-asking the question is still important.

Decisions needed quickly are valuable...plain and simple. Why? Shorter decision cycles translate to less risk of your invested time and capital. These decisions present a clearer path to completion. Conversely, decisions carrying extended time frames present more unknowns and generally greater time and expense commitments. They're also more prone to disruption and cancellation.

If there's no date for a decision, keep probing to discover why–what are the issues impacting the decision? Sometimes, the date is unknown because there is no commitment to act, the focus is just to evaluate. These are the accounts you want to avoid, until they have a date.

Quick decisions are a priority, while long-term opportunities get rationed blocks of time and effort.

Are the budget and the funding in place?

Much like the last question, these issues may seem very basic, however, they can represent insurmountable problems. In some markets, purchases that are not budgeted are rarely acted upon. Your proposal may require lengthy periods of time before it is included in an annual or quarterly budget plan. Then...the budget itself must be funded!

Winning orders that can't be placed because they lack financial resources is a costly waste of effort. The funding issue needs to be thoroughly explored. If the prospective purchaser has a financial challenge, you need to evaluate the risk of competing for their business, which may become non-existent. This issue can arise when prospects lose budget or suffer financial setbacks. Small businesses often rely on cash flow or credit lines to complete purchases, either of which can change quickly.

I can relate countless instances of transactions that evaporated after weeks or months of competitive effort. Financial issues can arise despite the size, reputed strength or brand name of the business. They can be temporary delays or permanent roadblocks. Don't assume purchasers, large or small, have the financial ability or commitment to consummate a contract just because they're shopping. Keep asking the question, and cut your exposure if the answer changes.

Do the math!

Try keeping track of the time and direct expenses you invest in a specific group of prospects for the next 6 months. The exercise will be eye opening. Quickly you will begin to question why some prospects are consuming significant amounts of time or why others are the source of so much travel, entertainment and other direct expenses.

Patterns will begin to emerge. Some prospects represent low-cost, high-return transactions. Others seem to be endless sources of expense with little return even after you finally win the business. How can you find more of the former and eliminate the later? It's a question every businessperson should begin to ask and then act upon.

Breaking the mindset of *any sale is a good sale* is difficult, but even a basic analysis will help you visualize and then intellectualize the concept. The discussion about providing seven presentations, and being asked for the eighth, opened my eyes to reality. You don't want to spend

$40,000 to make a $25,000 sale! Yet, it happens each and every business day.

Winning business by continually competing against long odds creates a high expense rate and results in a losing financial equation. It's why so many businesses fail despite having an impressive list of customers.

I can't afford to compete against only those people I know I can beat! This statement is often made with both sincere conviction and an equal amount of frustration. It reflects the challenge of competition and lies at the core of competing efficiently.

CASE STUDY
Competing Efficiently

Bob has been on the road making calls for three days. His list of appointments is finished. The results of the trip have been predictable; once again, he prevailed over Ace Pump and gained a brand new account; he lost to Western Pump in yet another close contest; and was a distant finisher against World Pump.

Ace is a classic Bottom Feeder. They sell inexpensive pumps and provide very little service to their customers. Their client base is surprisingly large but less than happy. Western Pump is a Mainstream with better results than Ace but trading on a reputation, which has eroded precipitously under its current ownership. They are much better at marketing than at product development or service. In fact, they purchase their motors from Ace, which is not a business policy they care to discuss or acknowledge. World Pump is the market's Gold Standard. They build good quality pumps, support them well; but, they're a high-price alternative. The current product line is in danger of becoming too expensive for the core marketplace.

Bob and his partner are ex-World Pump employees. Joe was the VP of Engineering and Bob served as VP of Sales for many years. They started their business to serve a market demanding quality pumps at reasonable purchase prices and on-going maintenance costs. They are in the first year of operation and it's proving to be a difficult struggle!

Bob is a long way from home and has a decision to make this evening. Should he drive home and go to the office in the morning or start calling on local suspects that don't fully meet his criteria as prospective customers? He knows his struggling new company needs more business opportunities to survive...maybe he should stay for another two days and try to discover a couple of long shots?

His conscience gets the best of him and he elects to stay on and work this territory. By noon on Saturday, he's exhausted and calls it a week! The last two days turned up responses like, *"I'll think about it!"* ... *"Call me next year!"* and a lot of polite *"No, thanks!"*

On the drive home, he's anxious about the requirement for more opportunities, but finds solace in knowing he put in a solid week of work. He resolves to keep turning over this territory and hope for the best. *"I have to find more deals where Ace and I are the finalists, just keep trying hard to beat the other two in each and every deal I can talk my way into."*

Joe is on the warpath! It's Monday and his partner just turned in his weekly expenses. *"You spent a week in Toledo and made one sale grossing $3,000. The travel and entertainment expenses alone were over $3,000. We can't afford many more trips like that!"*

Bob's anger and frustration caused him to snap at his partner. *"Hey, give me a break, I worked very hard last week! I didn't exactly enjoy taking ten people out to dinner, only to be told we lost again to World, or spending a full day trying to explain why our compressor motor is really stronger than Western's single-cycle unit. Do you have any idea how many rejections I got? I am trying my best, what do you want me to do?"*

"Bob, you need to do something because we are running out of time, and worst of all, we're running out of money!"

The decisions Bob made are very common approaches to competing for business. In truth, many enterprises compete themselves into ruin, just as Bob is doing. He is also learning that selling for Brand New is very different from life as a sales executive at Gold Standard. Suppose Bob had taken a different approach...

Bob shook hands with his newest customer. *"Do you know any Ace customers who could benefit from my product? We are willing to pay a significant referral fee for leads."*

His customer offered, *"There are two people here in town you should call, and tell them I suggested they meet with you."*

Bob did exactly that, and much to his surprise, wrote a new order on Monday afternoon. His new customer confided, *"Your timing is perfect, we open our new site next week and I really would like to avoid doing any more business with Ace!"*

From the second lead, Bob received a promise to decide on his product within 30 days. Bob's favorite question and offer became: *"Do you know any Ace customers who could benefit from my product? We are willing to pay a significant referral fee for leads."*

He was ready to celebrate the new week by emerging victorious, not once but twice, against Ace Pump. Bob planned to spend Tuesday competing against Western and their single-cycle pump. He knew this supposed feature was just marketing nonsense. He was going to take a stronger approach to debunking Western's claims.

His first offer was straightforward, *"Try our unit for 60 days, no obligation! If we don't meet your needs, I will personally pick the equipment up. If you're satisfied, all I ask is you agree to pay the invoice, give us a testimonial endorsement and take some reference calls."* Then he corrected his competitor, *"Please don't take this the wrong way, but you need to know the single-cycle motor isn't any different from every other manufacturer's pump motor. It's just a different way of describing a standard compression pump! In fact, it's manufactured by Ace Pump and identical to their unit!"*

"No obligation?"

"None, I want you to see the true power our motor can provide!"

"Manufactured by Ace?"

"Yes sir!"

A quick handshake, and the trial was underway. One more phone call to make...

"How am I doing with my proposal?"

"Well, we're leaning to World Pump, they seem to be a better fit for our business. Your company is quite new and we're not at all convinced you can give us the kind of global service we require. I'm not giving you a final no but you are really a long shot."

"I'm going to get out of the way on this project. I really think we can help you on a local scale. Are you willing to use our pump in a defined role at the Toledo facility?"

"What do you have in mind?"

"How about using us as temporary replacements when you have a failure or take the World units down for maintenance. Our pump is easy to install, inexpensive and its mean-time to failure far exceeds World's own standards."

"Interesting idea, call me next week, I may be interested in taking a single pump just to experiment with."

"I'm in town today. I can drop off a sample unit this afternoon!"

The drive home Tuesday evening was quick. Two orders, a 60-day trial and throw in a commitment to test a sample pump for back-up role at a major industrial corporation, made for a successful start to the week! Expenses for the trip were $750, sales of $6,000 (less a $150 referral fee) and three solid days to work the phones looked a lot more promising.

Bob reminded himself, *Wednesday morning, hit the phones to run down the other referrals to replace Ace and schedule the trial.* He made a note to create: a marketing plan to solicit the entire Ace client base with a series of special incentives; a strategy to co-exist with World Pump; and last but not least, a white paper authored by a respected and well-known engineer to demystify the single-cycle pump for his friends at Western to digest. Bob's inner voice told him, *Keep focusing on how to compete with each profile...Brand New challenges Mainstream by...Bottom Feeders clients are prime targets...Gold Standards don't like the rules to be changed...*

On his desk were two messages from late Tuesday evening:

"Excellent proposal! I spoke with your two new customers. Rather than wait for 30 days, just ship me a unit next week, we are looking forward to doing business with you and replacing Ace! I have several referrals for you, do they qualify for the $150 offer?"

"Call me tomorrow to discuss the pump which is being made by Ace for Western. We had a bad experience with Ace some years ago. I don't want to go down the same path again."

When Joe stopped at Bob's office Friday evening, his partner was gazing out the window, millions of miles away, while his phone was ringing.

"You doing okay?"

"Yeah, I was just enjoying the sound of momentum...been a long time coming!"

The challenge, *"I can't afford to compete against only those people I know I can beat!"* does not get resolved by competing directly against those that you can't beat!

Solve it by competing efficiently and concentrating on the best way to challenge each competitive profile you encounter. Competing efficiently includes carefully managing the use of your limited selling time and capital.

A business must compete to survive...
It must also survive to compete!

Competing for the sake of competition may instinctively feel right, but each and every contest has a cost attached. Spend your valuable time and money on the challenges you realistically expect to win.

Build on your successes! You may well discover that the adversaries you could not defeat five years ago, or last year, are now within your competitive reach.

TEST YOUR KNOWLEDGE

1. "I will compete anytime, anywhere, with anyone, for any opportunity!" is a dangerous competitive policy. True/False

2. Create a niche for your business around high-probability competitive contests you win again and again. True/False

3. These questions can help evaluate the cost of competing.
- **❑ What other vendors are you considering?**
- **❑ Is the funding in place?**
- **❑ How do you intend to reach a decision?**
- **❑ All the above.**

4. Think of your selling time as an investment. True/False

5. Spending $40,000 to win a $20,000 order is...
- **❑ Smart—because you have a new customer.**
- **❑ Efficient—because you could have spent more.**
- **❑ Effective—it kept you busy.**
- **❑ A mistake!**

6. Shorter decision cycles translate to less risk of your invested time and capital. True/False

7. It is safe to assume purchasers, large or small, have the financial ability and the commitment to consummate a contract because they're shopping. True/False

8. When a prospect doesn't know how they intend to reach a decision, which two of the following statements are true?
- **❑ They can alter the rules at any time in a way you can't accommodate.**
- **❑ They are on a fast track.**
- **❑ They need your consulting.**
- **❑ It's easy for them to change their minds.**

9. Winning business by continually competing against long odds creates a high expense rate. True/False

10. A business must compete to survive...it must also survive to compete! True/False

CHAPTER 8

Correcting Your Adversaries And Defending Your Proposals

Can I correct my adversaries without sounding negative? Should I ignore their attacks? Will my prospects mistake my silence for resignation? Important questions which lead to competitive challenges.

Most people do not like negative behavior. Each political election cycle, the debate about negative advertisements usually takes center stage. Survey after survey reports the practice is unpopular. So how come it keeps coming back again and again? The sad truth is that it works...especially if the response to it is clumsy or worse. Every business day, salespeople carry with them a list of competitive 'knock-offs' to use against adversaries. Crossing the line between fact and fiction leads to negative selling!

Negative selling, for our purposes, is defined as: *Making statements about a competitor that are factually inaccurate and intentionally communicated in an attempt to damage or diminish their proposal.* The statements often contain partial truths and questionable facts.

Competitive behavior is often punctuated with negative selling that exists across the full spectrum of competition profiles. Don't be surprised to discover negative selling goes beyond the domain of Bottom Feeders. This form of selling can be a conscious company strategy or the purview of individual salespeople or executives. Occasionally, the account in play can intentionally or inadvertently cause a sales environment to turn negative.

However you get to negative selling, the root cause is usually the same...someone's fear and desperation. It's a mistake to underestimate the power of either of these emotions or the impact they can have on the competitive environment.

We are going to discuss several strategic questions that all competitors will ultimately face. Under each question will be a series of tactical responses and our advice to diminish the impact of negative selling.

- **How should I correct my competitors?**
- **What is the best response to an attack?**
- **When do I present my rebuttal?**
- **What can I do to manage the competition?**

Strategic Question–How should I correct my competitors?

I use the word 'correct' intentionally to set the tone for this discussion. Corrections are about setting the record straight without becoming hostile or contemptuous, which a prospect can easily view as a personal rebuke.

"They said what?" This is the moment in time when you must decide if your sales efforts will turn negative or you'll exercise restraint. I will admit setting the record straight by launching your own counter attack may be momentarily satisfying! You do not, however, want to win a small 'feels good' argument and destroy a valuable opportunity as a result.

Start by reminding yourself to correct the competitor, not your prospect! Telling your prospect they're wrong or worse will not do much to build a relationship, or encourage an open dialogue. Nothing makes the challengers happier than your disagreement with your prospect over some information provided by the competition. The personality profiles we have discussed, especially B.A. Friend and Power Socializer, may not accept any criticism, no matter how inadvertent or mild it may be, without damaging your relationship.

Correcting misinformation, or conclusions that are incorrect, is especially difficult when your prospect has 'accepted' or 'agreed to' the material in question. Attacking the material can easily be interpreted as attacking the prospect. *"How could you believe this nonsense?"* or *"You have got the facts all wrong!"* can quickly become a personal affront.

Still, it's just as dangerous to ignore false assertions or factual errors in an effort to avoid an awkward moment. If you fail to correct these challenges, you may be surprised to find yesterday's false information becomes tomorrow's factual material! Prospects deserve the opportunity to hear your response to claims made by competitors. Interestingly, some prospects will encourage the exchange of claims and counter-claims. It's a way of discovering information. They reach verdicts based on your ability to present and defend the value of your products.

How do you correct the alleged facts? Start with a neutral statement.
—A lot of our prospects get confused about this issue. Let me try to clear it up...
—I don't want you to take this the wrong way, but I have a different view about...
—Can we revisit this topic because I suspect we hold different positions?
The statement should acknowledge that a potential for disagreement exists, yet display a sincere desire to discuss the issue, examine both views and work towards reaching agreement. Your voice and body language must not be angry, self-righteous, condescending or confrontational.
Dismiss the source of the incorrect information as being—confused, misinformed or just out of date. Don't become angry or attempt to blame the

supplier of the material for being disingenuous or worse. An even-keeled correction focused on setting the record straight is far more effective.

Portraying an adversary as a 'complete loser with no redeeming value' insults the prospect that is investing time and money exploring their proposal. You don't want a prospect to think, *"Do they hold me in the same low regard as the competitor?"*

Offer your competitor a compliment! "*They are excellent at... I admire the way they have...*" Demonstrate your ability to think and act independently. Prospects will respect the fact you are broad-minded enough to admit the competition offers value. This simple act will also give you the capital to correct the same competitor on important facts.

I can recall standing at the podium of a large conference room after being introduced to a group of senior executives. The sponsor of the meeting was charged with finalizing the recommendation for a very large and highly competitive project. The meeting was designed to allow his "Cs" and their staffs to ask questions and seek clarifications about my proposal. The first question addressed to me:

"Could you take as much time as necessary, and tell us why we should do business with you, rather than Smith Corporation?"

I started with a positive statement, *"My competitor is a fine company. They win business. We respect them as marketers. I also believe we offer a product with superior engineering and global support! Our product specifically meets the global needs of your business. Candidly, I would be more concerned about Smith's proposal if you were a smaller domestic manufacturer with less extensive requirements."*

"Will you respond to several specific criticisms they raised?"

"Certainly!"

"Have they hired 50% of your company's sales force in the last year?"

"Actually, they've hired one person, a good salesperson. The hire comprises 50% of their current sales force. We have 50 salespeople, they hired one!"

Some papers were shuffled...some chuckling!

"Was your product removed from Global Widget?"

"It was—the business was sold to new owners and they closed the production line in Europe. Dozens of other products were also discontinued. Actually, the acquiring company is a current client of ours. They will take reference calls...and verify the transaction."

"Is Smith trying to mislead us?"

"Well...I'd rather focus on how we can assist you in making your project a success. Smith's problem with the facts is an issue you will have to judge for yourself!"

The audience greeted my smile with acknowledgement and approval.

Tactical Response—Correct the big-picture issues.
Suppose your competitor has made two misstatements you must correct. The first correction was their failure to countersink the mounting screws on the proposed widgets. The second issue was a failure to disclose they had entered bankruptcy last week for the second time this decade. Which correction is most important for your prospect to understand? Okay, number two is the unanimous winner.

We all have a limited amount of information we can retain and a definite span of attention. Make certain that your corrections are those with the most impact and the broadest reach. Backing up a literal wheelbarrow and unloading every piece of competitive graffiti you can think of risks having just the opposite effect. Why? The details can become overwhelming and are often judged to be mundane competitive material.

The corrections you make should be communicated to your prospect clearly and concisely. Speaking in code and hoping your prospect gets the message is a mistake. *"I think she understood the message"* will not suffice. If the statement is important enough to correct, then it is imperative that your message be delivered clearly and understood completely.

Tactical Response—Negative selling does not work—don't do it!
Rumor-mongering, making unsubstantiated claims or distortions of the truth will cost you business. The reason is simple—once your missteps are exposed, you are left with diminished credibility. Every statement, every fact that you have presented is suspect. The prospect is left with the difficult decision of dismissing your proposal or taking the chance that other unpleasant surprises are waiting in the wings. In any case, your competitive position is substantially weakened.

The sales call started with a direct question:

"How well do you understand our competitor's product? Because once you understand, it you will never want to purchase it!"

What followed was a 30-minute diatribe of statements, allegations and unsubstantiated claims about the competitor. The prospect tried on several occasions to redirect the conversation, but undaunted, the attacker continued. The sales representative then concluded the presentation asking:

"Do you have any questions? I am sure you are much too smart to waste your time or money on my competitor! Can I write up the order for your signature?"

The prospect's answer was simple and pointed...

"Thanks for the information, unfortunately, I don't know anything about your solution, and we are out of time. I will call you if we need any thing else!"

They never did.

Do not be drawn into this trap by competitors who embrace slander as a way of selling their products. Colleagues describe this temptation as *"getting down and dirty"* with the competition! The end result is often neither participant prevails because the audience will not tolerate this behavior.

Have you ever won an order because the prospect is annoyed about the behavior of a competitor? Most salespeople have! Very often the annoyance can be summarized: *"They would not stop telling me what was wrong with the other company and they never told me about their product!"*

Sell your value and strengths, and correct the competitors. You will be rewarded with a clear conscience and more customers. Negative selling is a slippery slope to be avoided—its benefits are of dubious short-term value and of little long-term advantage.

Avoiding the trap of negative selling doesn't mean you should ever hesitate to compare your solution to the competition. It is, in fact, one of the most important messages you must communicate!

Tactical Response—Reveal the "Big News"!

During my sales career I sold in a marketplace that had two major players—my business and our competitor. Both companies were growing rapidly and were very equally matched except for one very critical issue: customer service! Simply put, we were focused on after-the-sale support and they were not. We always touted our excellence in this area and discussed the problem our competitor had candidly.

My first meeting with the decision maker at a new prospect was proceeding very well. I was listening to his needs and getting ready to make some intelligent comments when...a competitive lesson unfolded before me! My prospect announced: *"As you probably are aware your competitor has had some real issues with client support. We were delighted to have them come forward, admit to the problem and explain how they have reorganized the whole function to fix this serious issue—without our ever asking!"*

When you know what your competitors are going to say about your company, the product or yourself, beat them to it by *revealing*. This will increase your personal credibility and position their big news as just yesterday's information. Very few of us have the perfect business or product, without a blemish on our record. When you reveal, include an explanation of what happened and how you have corrected the problem. If the problem is still real, explain your plan to get it fixed.

You may also want to reveal issues that the competitors may not attack, but are real and likely to be discovered by your prospect. I call this "getting in front of the bad news".

I had great personal success with a product that my company recalled for poor quality! When I say that, people often chuckle but the complete story is all about revealing. Yes, the product was pulled from production and withdrawn from the market for several years before its re-introduction. The re-engineered version was carefully tested and quite efficient. Our competitors loved to regale how the product was a complete failure.

So here is what I did: *I approached my prospects by revealing the product's interesting history. Candidly, it was a failure—withdrawn and re-engineered at the cost of millions of dollars. Along the way, we came to understand how to make the product really efficient, cost effective and functional. We replaced the original product at each and every account with our new version.*

I would have the VP of Engineering take the prospect through the new version and our Customer Support VP go through the service track record. Finally, I provided several reference accounts—all of which had experienced the original failures and would speak to the new version. I sold dozens of units! In fact, most of my prospects were truly impressed with our commitment to get the product corrected.

My sales colleagues were mystified that anyone could sell even a single unit. Why? They were busy trying to avoid or hide from history— allowing the competition to deliver their 'big news' version of how the product failed, and only then trying to refute the attacks. It was a confusing charade that played right into the competition's strategy.

Tactical Response—When there are misunderstandings, blame your communication skills, not the prospect's ability to comprehend!

Walking to his car a frustrated business executive mutters, *"They just didn't understand...they didn't get it! That's why I lost this deal!"*

His partner, also frustrated, clears the air with a simple observation, *"You're right, they didn't get it—because you did a terrible job of explaining it!"*

The responsibility for being sure your prospects understand 'it' rests on you! Learning to communicate effectively is imperative. I suggest you take some time and invest in studying the art of communication by reading several of the countless books on this subject. Everybody fails to communicate on occasion; it's part of the human condition. The challenge is to keep the failures to a minimum by constantly working to improve.

Blaming your communication skills also removes a burden from your prospects. Rather than tell them they don't understand, take them off the hook by blaming yourself. This selfless act will allow you to try a second or third time to get your points across, without damaging the relationship.

Tactical Response—It's okay to answer a question with a simple *"I don't know the answer!"*

Which of these two scenarios would you prefer?

Two prospects leave your office and exchange puzzled looks. The first prospect remarks, *"I can't believe the answer he gave to your question was correct, it defies logic, basic physics and seems ridiculous! Is he lying to us or is he just incompetent?"*

Same two prospects, same scenario. *"I wish he could have answered your question, but he was honest enough to admit he didn't know the answer. Let's wait to see if he comes back with a response."*

It's a mistake to guess at the answers to questions, and unconscionable to lie. The *"I don't know!"* response is refreshingly candid and will do wonders for your credibility. Prospects want to trust the vendors they do business with. Everyone understands very few people can answer any and every question.

It is not unusual to be asked questions when the inquirer already knows the answer. I once received an order and while being congratulated was assured my success was the reward for answering a series of trick questions with a simple, *"I don't know"* and following up with, *"We can't do that."* The prospect later confided they got quite a laugh out of some of the incredible stuff my competitor gave as an answer.

Prospects have a right to expect answers, but no one expects to receive all those answers immediately. Be certain to follow up on your promise to give them a well-reasoned and thoughtful response.

Tactical Response—Be 100% factual in your corrections.

This is really important! Don't correct your competitor's misstatements with your own misstatements. Prospects get really unnerved about this kind of behavior. I refer to it as *"snatching defeat from the jaws of victory!"* Unfortunately, it's a common competitive error. Why? The urgency of correcting a misstatement becomes so overwhelming and personal that the need to deliver a thoughtful and accurate response is overridden by the urge to strike back.

If the competition has made an error or accusation about your business or product, set the record straight with 100% accuracy. When you speak about a competitor's business or product, be certain your information is 100% accurate or just don't comment.

The Competitor's Resume will assist you in getting the facts correct. It also should remind you of the value of insisting your competitive information is kept current and accurate.

Tactical Response—If you do make an error, correct your mistake!
The quicker you set the record straight, the better. Most prospects realize an occasional error is part of the competitive process. Their concern becomes alarm when the mistakes become frequent and are allowed to stand. Don't put your prospects in the position of questioning if the errors are honest mistakes or intentional misrepresentations. *"I made an error"* may be embarrassing, but the consequence of being suspected of intentional misrepresentations is much worse.

Correcting an adversary is difficult and necessary. Don't be surprised or dismayed if your prospect does not agree with or accept your rebuttals. Your goal is to present the corrections accurately, and have them acknowledged.

Agreement is a reward you may not always be able to achieve. Fortunately, winning business does not require every decision maker, recommender or evaluator to agree with every position, explanation or offer made in your proposal. They just have to agree your value is the best solution for them personally and for their business!

Strategic Question—What is the best response to an attack?

Every businessperson has or will compete with an adversary who functions in one mode...the attack mode! They are relentless and driven by raw emotion. Their goal is not to correct your proposal, but simply to destroy it and you! The attacks may be personal or driven by some claim of righteous indignation. They may even continue long after your adversary is eliminated from consideration.

The danger you face is that the prospect may, understandably, dismiss both the attacker and attacked just to be rid of the headache. Perhaps the most troubling outcome occurs when the prospect accepts the allegations as being factual. When negative selling plays on a prospect's fears, emotions and predispositions, it can be a challenge to overcome.

I have found several approaches to deflect these types of attacks. Whichever approach you choose, keep your conversation casual and self-reflective. Don't display anger or hostility towards the substance of the attack or the attacker.

First, if you know the behavior is likely to occur, reveal!
"I regret telling you this, but you need to know, General Contracting has a real history of negative selling. Unfortunately, I am usually the target of their tirades. It just seems to be their response to the pressure of competing for business! I want you to know, I'm not going to make it worse by responding to their bad behavior!"

Second, turn the behavior pattern against your adversary.
"It's unfortunate this is how they prefer to do business. We respect our prospect's and customer's judgment and common sense. Our focus is on providing value and service, not on discrediting our competitors."

Finally, remind your prospect negative selling is about fear. Ask the prospect to consider: Why is the attacker afraid of your proposal? Why are they avoiding a discussion primarily focused upon the value of their solution? Is it because they know their product will not pass the scrutiny of a careful purchase evaluation?

You have secured the moral high ground and called any claims the adversary has made into question! Even if they stop the negativity and attacks, their credibility has been wounded.

Strategically, you will not succeed in responding to personal attacks by demonstrating you can outdo your attacker's negative selling with your own negative campaign. Learning to resist the trap of responding in kind will position you and your business as credible and responsible future business partners. Concentrate your efforts on *correcting* your adversary's misstatements and sell the strength and value of your proposal!

Tactical Response—Don't accommodate a prospect that encourages a negative selling environment.
Occasionally, a prospect will set the stage for negative selling. They will encourage or demand you 'spill the dirt' on the competitors or demon-

strate you intend to 'scrap for their business'. I can't honestly recall having lost any business because I refused to accept the invitation.

These efforts are often misguided or just wrongheaded attempts at exerting control. The behavior is typical of Evaluators, and occasionally a Recommender, who are inexperienced or unfamiliar with competitive evaluations. I have seen prospects quickly back away from these demands when I politely refused to accommodate the request.

Customers need to purchase products that meet their needs. Selecting your product primarily because an adversary has reputed problems with theirs is a pyrrhic victory. Winning a deal today by engaging in negative selling provides you tomorrow's ideal candidate for a problem. Those who choose your solution because the alternatives were reported to be inadequate, unfortunately, often decide in time that what they chose was also unsatisfactory!

Take the high ground even if the prospects encourage negative selling.

Strategic Question—When do I present my rebuttal?

The challenge is to avoid the two extremes—being too early or waiting until it's too late. Early corrections may be wasted on competitors that were going to be eliminated regardless of your information.

Ted knocked on the door of the prospect's office and quickly slipped into a chair. He was anxious to correct several allegations Wilcox Industries had made about his product.

"I want to clarify some misinformation you have been given about our S6500 Moving Stairway platform. Wilcox always seems to make a number of claims about our product, which are inaccurate. It's too bad, but they seem to spend more time discussing our solution then selling their own product."

The prospect put down his glasses and sighed.

"Ted, I hope you didn't make this trip just to talk about Wilcox."

"Why?"

"We have no interest in their escalators. Their product is outdated and their sales approach is just as stale. I have other things I have to finish today. Call me next week and we can get together."

The meeting was over and accomplished very little.

Unfortunately, waiting until you have been informed of your elimination is also a mistake. Whatever corrections you belatedly attempt to put in front of the prospect are likely to be viewed as the sour grapes of a failed competitor.

Begin making competitive corrections when you have reached the point in the prospect's evaluation process where vendor eliminations are imminent or if you feel the misinformation is becoming a serious problem.

Most prospects will gather information about a number of businesses and possible solutions to fulfill their needs. They will then begin to reduce the solutions under consideration until they arrive at a select group of final options. Selecting the winner may be days or weeks in the future, but some vendors are going home immediately. It's at this moment that prospects can be persuaded to accept or reject specific competitors.

Understanding how your prospect intends to make a decision (a topic discussed in Chapter 7) gives you a significant advantage. It alerts you to the right moment to present your rebuttal, and the person who needs to hear this important message.

Although correcting the misstatements made by competitors is very important, the main focus of your selling challenge is to present clearly the value your product provides. Don't become so fixated on issuing corrections that you forget to establish firmly your own product's selling message. Winning business is about presenting a positive message. Value and strong relationships trump sales campaigns built on others' failings and negative behavior.

Smart competitors start by understanding a prospects needs and then communicating the value they offer to satisfy those needs. They explain the outstanding features, functions and services that are part of their solution. The discussion includes disclosure of what is unique about the product they provide, along with an explanation of why their approach is in the best interest of the prospect. "This is why I can provide for your needs better than anyone else!"

When you distinguish why you are unique and how you provide a better alternative, in a positive and fact-oriented conversation you build credibility. Prospects want and need to know why they should choose your solution. Tell them what differentiates your product and business from the competition!

Focus on what you do, why you have carefully selected a particular approach and why it is important to solving their needs, and your message will resonate.

The primary goal of every salesperson is to persuade the prospect that your product provides the value they need and must have in order to advance their business.

Tactical Response—Let the prospect tell you when the rebuttal should be presented.
If you are uncertain when a rebuttal needs to take place, ask the Executive Buyer this question: *"I'd like to correct some misinformation you have been given by my competitor. It's important for you to have this material before you make any decisions. When should we plan on having this discussion, and who would you like to be in attendance?"*

The answer you receive will tell you where the decision process stands and how you are doing. I have had responses range from "*You need to do this now!*" to *"There's really no rush...we need another month before any decisions are discussed."*

As a safety check, address the same question to the individual you have identified as a Recommender and everyone else the Executive Buyer acknowledged. Compare the answers you receive and be prepared to keep asking this question if the responses are inconsistent.

Strategic Question—What can I do to manage the competition?

Successful competitors learn to manage the competition by influencing the prospects with the responsibility for making a decision. Influence by its very definition is subtle and difficult to measure...yet we all know it exists.

In order to exercise influence, you must be both respected and viewed as a person who can deliver valuable insight and information to the individual attempting to reach a decision. As you introduce yourself and your product throughout The Selling Pyramid, keep in mind:

- First impressions count.
- Establish your credentials.
- Build a mutual relationship.
- Focus on discovering, understanding and then meeting the prospect's needs.
- Communicate your message in a clear and straightforward style.
- Accountability and responsible behavior will earn you trust and respect.

Use your influence carefully—it comes in limited quantities.

The best use of influence is persuading the prospect your value can best provide for their needs. Your leadership efforts should attempt to keep the focus of the evaluation process on your product. Why? You want to be accepted and anointed as part of a prospect's team. The quicker you are viewed as a valuable asset, the more difficult you become to dislodge...product issues aside! This doesn't mean the prospect will overlook serious product issues, or a weak business proposal, but you will be given a margin of error to correct challenges that other competitors will not enjoy.

Tactical Response–Keep the competitors out of the spotlight!
The more visibility your competitors have, the greater their opportunity to find a supportive audience. Making them the target of your sales attention increases their visibility, without any effort on their part! Let them earn their way to the spotlight by the merits of their own effort.

I received a call from an executive at a major manufacturing firm who asked if I could be available for a meeting. He revealed that despite their reservations about interviewing another potential new supplier for a critical project, they wanted the opportunity to meet with us because our competitors had made a concerted effort to point out our failings. "We are suspicious of the amount of effort they have devoted to telling us why we should not do business with you." Our competitors literally led this opportunity to our door! Two lessons follow:

Attacking your competitors, without provocation, can easily arouse the suspicions of your prospect. Many people will surmise the attacks are the result of genuine fear of your adversary's product, or that you are a businessperson who thrives on negative selling. Neither portrait paints a favorable picture.

Second, it has never been lost on me that sometimes the very companies you most want to avoid get left off the list of potential challengers. Advertising the names of the companies you normally compete with, or most fear, before you know they are even under consideration is a mistake. Remember the old saying, *"Let sleeping dogs lie"*? If this happens 10% of the time, you may get a nice bump in business.

Tactical Response–The toughest competitor is...
I always enjoyed being asked that question by a prospect. My answer is always the same–*they are all tough competitors!* Then, I use the opportunity to talk about positive things that relate to my business and products. I am not in the business of trying to recommend competitors or advising my prospects what other products they should consider. Experience has

shown that this common question is often a test to see if you exhibit fear of a specific competitor or will turn negative. Do not take the bait and turn the spotlight on!

Tactical Response—Don't recommend a competitor!
Should you acknowledge or even recommend them? Some professionals will always acknowledge a competitor that is a weak alternative. The problem I have with this approach is that it's less than fully candid. Your prospect may, in fact, know or learn that you have omitted other key adversaries. In either case, you have been compromised! The simple way to prevent this problem is to reveal all the competitors or none. My recommendation is to reveal none and acknowledge they are all tough. Later go back and find out who is under consideration.

Tactical Response—You never know who is listening!
Always assume the competition is listening. The discussions you have about competitive strategy, your best accounts, contests you are winning or losing, and product information are confidential. Don't hold these discussions in public or make the false assumption you're conversations not being overheard! I have overheard conversations on airplanes, in elevators, office building lobbies and busy restaurants that changed the course of an opportunity I was competing to win. Most experienced sales executives can recount similar stories. Make sure your important discussions are kept private. If you are in doubt...keep quiet!

Tactical Response—It's the finish line that matters!
One of the lessons of Part II is...some competitive business opportunities start with your opponents being the preferred choice. In other competitive sales, you may fall out of favor along the way. As business people gain experience, the idea of trailing in a competitive contest becomes less traumatic.

The product you sell may have a short or long sales cycle. The decision process may include a gradual elimination of competitors or have milestones that represent points for the dismissal of vendors. You always work to avoid elimination and execute your account plan to a sales methodology. I recommend reading ***Smart Selling! Your Roadmap to Becoming a Top Performer***. This book provides a complete discussion about the importance of developing a sales methodology.

Until the decision to purchase is recommended, approved and executed, there is no first place or second place. You may or may not be someone's favorite or the preferred choice of a certain group—all those positions can change quickly and often will. Don't take encouragement from or be dismayed as the result of the temporary pecking order. The finish line is what matters—not who leads the race at each step along the way!

Managing the competition is achievable! You start by establishing influence, using this influence in a positive way and exercising leadership. Contribute to the prospect's undertaking and earn yourself a place on their team. The only loser from this approach is your competition!

TEST YOUR KNOWLEDGE

1. Making statements about a competitor that are factually inaccurate and intentionally communicated in an attempt to damage or diminish is called...

2. Corrections are about setting the record straight without becoming hostile or contemptuous. True/False

3. The following tactics will help you correct competitors...
   - ❑ Negative selling does not work–don't do it!
   - ❑ Reveal the "Big News"!
   - ❑ Correct the big-picture issues.
   - ❑ All of the above.

4. When prospects can't understand or comprehend, it's okay to blame them. True/False

5. Never admit to a prospect you don't know the answer to a question! True/False

6. If a prospect encourages negative selling, take the gloves off and give them what they want! True/False

7. Keep the competitors out of the spotlight because...
   - ❑ Making them the target of your attention increases their visibility.
   - ❑ The more visibility they have, the greater is their opportunity to find a supportive audience.
   - ❑ Let them earn their own way to the spotlight.
   - ❑ All of the above.

8. Successful competitors manage their opposition by influencing the prospect's decision makers. True/False

9. Don't become so fixed on correcting your competitors that you fail to establish your selling message. True/False

10. What is the best response to a competitor's attack?

....

....

....

CHAPTER 9

Bring A Winning Attitude!

What sets some business people apart from the competition?
They bring a winning attitude to the contest, reinforced by positive behavior, demeanor and body language. Their confidence, competency and experience as competitors confirm their expectation of winning. They may not always succeed, but they will be taken seriously and respected for their efforts. Their adversaries and prospects know they are a force and presence to be reckoned with!

Prospects respond to leadership, competency and other character strengths. Why? They want to be sure the purchase decisions they have made are in competent hands, which will protect their personal and business interests.

These ten characteristics can help you to develop a winning attitude and stand out from the competition:

- **Work Hard for the Order**
- **Keep Asking for the Business**
- **Fearlessness**
- **Persistence**
- **Positive...Positive...Positive**
- **Communicate**
- **Share your Knowledge**
- **Respect their Time**
- **Demonstrate Credibility**
- **Provide Leadership**

Our discussions will help you quickly grasp the power of every attribute and increase your ability to project a winning attitude in the competitive arena.

Work Hard for the Order

Everyone enjoys knowing someone is working hard to earn his or her business. Why? Working hard for an order sends two messages: *You are important to me! ... I am willing to invest my time and extraordinary effort meeting your needs!* Who would not be comforted by this behavior? Conversely, most people are thoroughly annoyed when they discover a businessperson is not willing to work for their business.

How does one demonstrate a willingness to work hard for an order? Tell your prospect you intend to work hard and then do it! Proactively assist them in the process of gathering information, becoming educated and resolving questions. *"Let me get you some material to explain"... "I can research that question for you."*

Whenever you commit to perform a task, attend a meeting or deliver helpful information, be certain to keep your promise. Prospects are attuned to how well you keep promises and commitments. They correctly presume that if you fail to meet your assurances before you have a sale, it's a bad omen for what will happen when the sale is complete. Broken promises can be interpreted as poor organization, a lack of concentration or not caring about the prospect's needs.

If the business is important enough to compete for...go the extra mile to earn a victory! Your commitment and diligence will pay real dividends.

Keep Asking for the Business

Prospects need to be assured you want their business without any doubts or hesitancy. The act of competing is time consuming and expensive. It's a serious and important obligation—you want to win the business you have chosen to pursue. Don't keep your intention a secret, share it with all your prospects! Remind them after meetings, telephone calls and in closing e-mails that you want their business. Each and every person you call on across the Selling Pyramid needs to hear this plea. Unfortunately, too few businesspeople take the extra time to emphasize this simple but powerful message.

Early in my sales career, a senior executive confided to me, *"I am not convinced you have the best product, but it was clear you really wanted our business, which is why you were selected."*

The next time you are in a tight contest, ask yourself if everybody understands beyond any doubt—you want their business. It only takes one person in a quandary to fall back on this message and give you the order, because they knew you really wanted the business. Careers and companies can turn on just one order!

Fearlessness

If you are expecting to fail, you will! So many competitive contests are won or lost because someone acted and someone else did not. The extra telephone call, the visit with an executive buyer, a challenge to a skeptical prospect, time spent with a purchasing agent others avoided—the results of rising above your fears.

When you expect to win, the difficult tasks become challenges to be undertaken, not shirked. The more thorny people and issues you engage, the further the envelope is pushed, the greater your comfort zone expands. The fear of failing and being rejected is the roadblock, which limits the ability to compete fully for business.

Ask yourself these two questions: Why not me? Are my self-imposed limitations preventing the success I deserve? Perhaps you need to learn new business skills, sales skills, presentation techniques and how to communicate effectively. Improving these important skills can be accomplished with hard work and dedication.

What most of us stumble over is an inability to get beyond our own comfort zones. Remind yourself, if it can be done by anyone else, you can do it! It's also okay to try what some may view as the impossible. You'll discover the impossible occasionally turns out to be very achievable—if you are willing to put fear aside.

What happens if I fail or am rebuffed? The results are much less painful or embarrassing than you may imagine. We all fail! You will be rebuffed, have telephones hung up, meetings refused, and endure rude behavior. When you accept failure as a learning experience, find humor in the moment and go right back to trying once again, the result is growth.

Prospects find personal assurance by choosing businesspeople exhibiting fearlessness. Their intuition tells them the same fearlessness will be put to work advocating their interests when they become a customer.

Persistence

Winning competitive orders is often long and difficult. The ability to weather the ups and downs along the way is a test of your desire to prevail. Many prospects subscribe to a competitive theory best summarized as: *"Only the persistent need apply—we're not easy to do business with!"* They view their business and its environment as tough and demanding, their vendors need to demonstrate the same tenacity. Competitors who want easy victories are not welcomed.

Persistence also gives you the aptitude to keep putting your fearlessness to the test. Securing the meeting you want with an Executive Buyer may well require multiple attempts and include several rebuffs. Making the extra call, providing an extra specification or report, all require more effort. Persistence gives you the resolve to keep pushing forward when other competitors give up and retreat.

Many prospects will not make it easy to earn their trust or business without large doses of determination. The competitive match is designed to be a test of your persistence!

Positive...Positive...Positive

If you believe you can win, you are destined to succeed. This achievement may not be attained every time you compete, but it will be realized. Positive people are also realists who understand they are ultimately responsible for creating success through learning and constantly developing new business skills.

Be certain your interactions with prospects have nothing but positive overtures. If this requires some work or reinforcement on your part, make the investment. A single negative performance will not go unnoticed; several will get you eliminated from consideration. No one will benefit more from your negative discussions or performances than your competitors.

I have always believed people are naturally attracted to positive energy. We all want to be associated with those who see and believe in striving to be the best they're capable of imagining. Positive energy is contagious and inspiring. Your prospects understand this phenomenon!

I recently lost a friend who was the very epitome of positive thinking and action. A successful developer who built projects across the globe, he always thought that whatever went wrong in his life or business was always 'good' or 'for the best'. Failures were just mistakes destined to be dismissed ultimately with a shake of the head and a smile! His humor was always intact and despite failing health, he never uttered a phrase that was not positive. When his heart started to fail in his late 80's, he joked his doctor wanted to put in a pacemaker built by the low-cost bidder. He had countless friends and admirers as those who exemplify a positive life always do!

Communicate

Provide information by speaking or writing. It's difficult to expect people to select solutions they can't comprehend and value. Yet, their ability to reach a favorable judgment is often predicated on your ability to communicate!

Think before you speak, every communication should have a goal. What do you want to achieve? What message do you want to convey? Forget the old adage about the importance of talking. The first rule of communication is to *listen!*

Listening leads to learning and asking open-ended questions. The more you learn about what your prospect needs and wants, the better you can tailor your presentations to reaching a mutual understanding of how you can meet those needs.

Speak clearly in understandable words and concentrate on your audience. Making eye contact with your listeners is very important; it verifies your attention and interest. Respond to questions with direct, sensible and truthful answers. Being evasive, engaging in double talk or rambling are all mistakes. Unfortunately, the message you convey is simple..."I have something to hide" or some reason to lie.

Good communication skills will allow you to create an atmosphere of trust and mutual respect with your prospect. You'll both achieve your goals when this type of relationship exists.

Your communications with prospects should include reaching an agreement on the next step. Every conversation, meeting or email needs to have a follow-on agreement. "*This is what we agree should be done next!*" This simple step will do wonders to keep your proposal moving toward closure and success.

Every act of sales communication should accomplish four objectives:

- Achieve the goal you set for the event
- Result in learning by both parties
- Help to build a relationship
- Reach agreement on the next step.

Master competitors have invested significant time and effort honing their ability to communicate. You must too!

Share your Knowledge

Prospects want to work with businesspeople knowledgeable about products, markets, industries, economic issues and business in general. They want the benefit of experience and wisdom. It's comforting to know the people you choose to do business with are experts in a market, industry or product. Prospects will often choose this zone of comfort over many other attributes! Conversely, they'll be nervous about selecting competitors who lack prerequisite wisdom or experience.

How willing are you to undertake the hard work and education required to become an expert in your field? The sooner you start on a path to learning your business and your prospect's, the quicker the competitive dividends will arrive. Savvy competitors will use their foundational know-how to set themselves apart from less experienced adversaries.

Respect their Time

Amateurs often just visit with prospects; polished competitors deliver information and value every time they meet with or talk to a prospect.

The difference is real and discernable. The best competitors respect a prospect's time constraints because they value their own time! The vast majority of prospects (specifically Achievers and Analytics) functioning as Cs, Executive Buyers or even Recommenders will not tolerate people wasting their time. Those who make this mistake are not welcomed back a second time.

Effective selling and competing is ultimately about setting goals, taking actions to reach those specific goals, and measuring the results in a continuum. When you embrace this mindset, the concepts of limited selling time, and respect for time, come into sharp focus. Deliver value whenever you interact with a prospect and your contributions will be welcomed and respected.

Demonstrate Credibility

The quality of being believable sets some competitors apart! The synonym for credibility is trustworthiness. There are dozens of actions and personal characteristics, which can be called credibility builders.

Here are several to consider:
–Be honest enough to tell a prospect, *"I don't know the answer!"* People are often suspicious of others who always have an answer to any and every imaginable question. It's refreshingly honest to admit you need help answering a question and then following through on your commitment.

–Admit to and correct your mistakes! It requires courage to correct an error. Prospects realize in complex competitive contests that errors are going to occur. It's part of their job to catch mistakes and re-examine the issues surrounding them. When you demonstrate you also believe it's your job to correct misstatements, they will conclude you are competing fairly and honestly, errors aside. Attempting to hide your mistakes, and ultimately being discovered, gets you eliminated from consideration.

–Tell prospects you can't meet a specific requirement! Disclosing will often result in...*"Okay, but..."* You can discuss why this requirement is beyond the scope of your offering, and present an alternative, if any, to the request. The prospect may decide to continue consideration of your proposal or move on. If they choose to continue, you're in a stronger position for having engaged in honest disclosure.

–Demonstrate open and fair-minded thinking. Prospects expect you to recommend and endorse your product. Be cautious presenting scripted sales dialogues; they can create an impression of highly partisan behavior and thinking. "*All she will do is give you the company line*" is a faint endorsement or evaluation. The ability to discuss your competitor's offerings, and your own, in a practical way with a fair-minded attitude will create credibility. "*We're a better solution, but their product has some unique features,*" or "*I can appreciate your dilemma, the competition has a good product.*"

—Keep the prospect's success as first and foremost. When the triumph of your prospect is your first demonstrated priority, you'll earn credibility. It's not difficult for most of us to discern quickly who is working on our behalf and who is not. The 'it's all about me' competitors are viewed as being capable of selfishly saying or doing anything to win an order. Not exactly an ideal environment to inspire credibility! You serve your own interest when you learn to put your prospect's success before your own!

—Work to a plan or methodology. No one likes to be an experiment or wants to select a disorganized business partner. If you present a disorganized competitive effort, you'll annoy most prospects. It's easy for them to dismiss your proposal because they lack confidence in your credibility and doubt you'll perform to their standards after the sale. Develop a business methodology that becomes your step-by-step roadmap to presenting products and winning new customers. The best competitors have learned to win by building personal credibility.

Provide Leadership

Competitors with a winning attitude provide guidance and direction. This final characteristic places their competitive strengths front and center.

They have the ability and confidence to lead an audience to discover, accept and embrace the value they represent...which in turn helps to create and reinforce their winning attitude. Leaders must have followers and prospects are willing to follow because they perceive it to be in their best interest. Leaders demonstrate to prospects the winning attitude we have discussed, which often tips the competitive decision in their favor.

Leadership skills can be developed through education, practice and unwavering commitment to personal and professional growth. Becoming a leader is the final step to achieving an unbeatable winning attitude...

TEST YOUR KNOWLEDGE

1. What sets some business people apart from the competition?
   - ❑ They are older.
   - ❑ They bring a winning attitude.
   - ❑ They don't worry about winning or losing.
   - ❑ The competition is afraid of them.

2. Prospects enjoy knowing someone is working hard to earn their company's business. True/False

3. Don't hesitate to ask for a prospect's business. True/False

4. Which of the following is true about the phrase: "If you believe you can win, you are destined to succeed!" ...
   - ❑ It means you are dangerously optimistic.
   - ❑ The motto reflects a positive attitude.
   - ❑ This attitude sets you up to fail.
   - ❑ Following this advise prevents any negative performances.

5. Every act of sales communication should achieve which two of the following results:
   - ❑ Deliver a pleasing message;
   - ❑ Achieve the goal you set for the event;
   - ❑ Include being evasive or engaging in double talk;
   - ❑ Reach agreement on the next step.

6. Prospects want to work with businesspeople who are knowledgeable about products and markets. True/False

7. Explain the characteristic of fearlessness.

   ....

   ....

8. The best competitors respect a prospect's time because they value their own time. True/False

9. Keeping your prospect's success first and foremost enhances credibility. True/False

10. Leaders must have followers! Prospects are willing to follow because...

CHAPTER 10

Final Thoughts...

Why Are Some Competitors So Difficult?

I would like to believe the competition is so difficult because they have followed our recommendations and learned how to prevail with a high degree of certainty! I also know, unless you act to prevent their success, your competitors will not and should not relent!

We keep losing to them!
The first reaction many business people have is: *Why is this happening to us?* The question is often followed by a litany of excuses, frustration, angst, and finger pointing. The assignment of blame is then punctuated by promises to do better. This form of relief is usually effective until the inevitable next loss occurs!

The real question is—What should be done immediately to change this reality? Difficult competitors will not relent when they have found a weakness to exploit. They will be delighted to maintain their favorable status quo!

The change question must lead to a thorough examination of how you are competing with this difficult adversary. Start with **The Competitor's Resume** and work through each detailed question and issue. Focus on concrete facts and discard what you may wish or hope to hear. Asking the prospects that have selected your opponent to share their evaluations and reasoning can be very enlightening.

Put yourself in the opponent's position and gain a step-by-step appreciation of how you are being beaten. This is a painful but essential exercise. No one enjoys being on the losing end of a contest...much less being regularly defeated!

Once you understand their game plan and why it works, you're now ready to take one of several actions:

- Change the terms of the competition.
- Vacate the market space.

Let's use a baseball analogy. If you are a pitcher who throws a fastball down the middle of the plate whenever you face a particular batter, and he or she proceeds to deliver the pitch into the grandstands time and time again, you may want to consider a different pitch! This is better known as changing the terms of the competition.

I can't tell you what change to make, but I will tell you to be certain the adjustment is both meaningful and quickly executed. Band-Aids do not cure broken bones! You may have to experiment with and implement a stage-by-stage competitive transformation until you get the results you want. The pace of competition has so accelerated in most markets you no longer have the luxury of slow and indecisive adjustments to strategy! Survival does truly go to those who can respond in a quick and nimble genre.

Niche products and businesses are popular current topics and a well-accepted approach to strategic positioning. When you niche, you focus on specific markets or products and abandon others. One of our basic tenets is you don't compete against those you can't dominate. The advice cuts two ways! Vacate market space you can't control or change your competitive strategy and regain dominance.

Leaving a market is always a difficult task. Unfortunately, far too many businesses have been lost because of a refusal to abandon unprofitable products and markets. Domination starts and grows by consistently winning business over your competitors. If you can't find a dominant competitive position in a marketplace, it may be time to move your resources.

Isn't competition really about pricing?

Pricing can drive competition. Certain markets and market segments can be extraordinarily price sensitive. The interesting truth about pricing, in my opinion, is often misunderstood.

- The role of price in the decision to purchase is often not paramount.
- Lower prices do not always prevail.

Price is a component in the decision process that both consumers and business purchasers undertake. Can you personally imagine only selecting products that had the cheapest price for each and every purchase decision? There may well be many circumstances when you will choose to select the lowest priced offering available, but every time you purchase?

Most consumers and business people balance price, quality, service, safety, performance, convenience and dozens of other product and business issues each time they make a decision to purchase. They want the best goods or services with the most favorable terms and conditions available at the time of purchase.

Rushing to fill a major order at 8 am, the shipping department was confronted with a disaster! This critical new order had to ship at noon or cancel. Unfortunately, the nail guns used to crate the merchandise had both failed. No crating—no shipping—no major order! Calls to the preferred supplier of the tool produced a promise to air-freight replacements that would arrive in 24 hours.

A secondary supplier can deliver nail guns within the hour, but his price is twice as much as the replacement from your preferred vendor. The available nail gun fully meets the shipping departments required specifications. The secondary supplier adamantly refuses to reduce his price, which is why he is the secondary supplier!

What would you have done? Lose the order for want of replacement nail guns? Refuse to pay the higher price? Perhaps you would have taken the merchandise that was immediately available!

Pricing is also directly tied to the uniqueness of a product. For example, commodity offerings such as #2 lead pencils or laser printer paper have far more commonality than a custom-designed and built conference table. The closer products get to 'standardized', the more important price becomes. It makes perfect sense that there is less to compete over, so pricing rises in importance.

Let's go back to our #2 pencils, a commodity right? Would you drive 20 miles to buy a box at a 5% discount? Or would you go to a local store with a little higher price and a very convenient location? Perhaps your cost of gas and time alone will more than offset the 5% differential. Suppose I told you the price differential amounted to 3 cents! Even commodity products are not wholly purchased because of price.

Customized offerings are even more difficult to evaluate in terms of value for the proposed price. Let's say you build custom-made cherry wood conference tables. The finished tables are generally regarded as works of art and true collectors' pieces. Your pricing becomes very elastic if you can truly establish unique value in the mind of your potential customers. Customized and unique always exact a premium price. In fact, most consumers and business entities understand and accept this marketplace reality.

Buyer behaviors are complex and mercurial. They are impacted by an untold number of mitigating issues. Unfortunately, the challenge of competition can't be overcome with a simple pricing exercise.

The competition is not a problem because...I don't have any!
I would like to dispel one last myth. Despite claims to the contrary, 99% of all business ventures have competition! Do you really believe that anyone could create a successful business, achieve customer recognition, generate cash flow and be ignored by the millions of business people focused on their own survival and prosperity? Not very likely! In fact, if you do not have a competitor it is because:

- You have a very temporary window before the onslaught begins!
- Your idea or concept has yet to evolve into a business or product.
- There is no established or even nascent market for your product or service.
- You are ignoring the existence of real challengers.

In my own experience, *ignoring* is the most common issue many business people hide behind or misinterpret. *"You see, our product is different from everyone else, so we don't have a real competitor!"* In reality, the very people who buy the solution will often dispute the claim of uniqueness. *"Yes, it's different, but the difference is not significant."... "It is a unique approach, but the end result is little different than several other vendors' solutions!"*

If a prospect can satisfy a need (which is essentially the same need you fulfill) by selecting an alternative product, you have a real competitor. For example, baby diapers can be made of cloth, paper or a synthetic material, but they essentially serve the same need–keep baby dry and clean! How a product solves a need, or is packaged, priced and promoted is important, but not an exemption from the actuality of competition.

Many business people will tell you that if you do not have a competitor, you do not have a business! The idea for a new product may be truly unique, but until the product comes to market, its competitive status can't be fully tested. The world is full of interesting solutions to non-existent needs. I believe you validate products in new or existing marketplaces by generating sales...which attracts competitors!

The Future...

I am sure you have concluded the competitive arena is complex and difficult. The rewards for succeeding as a competitor are significant, as are the consequences of failing! The reality of 'winners grow and losers go' reaches a finale very quickly.

The creation of new products, markets and industries continues to accelerate faster and faster. The pressure and challenge of ongoing competitive struggles will also continue to gather speed. Global barriers will shrink and all but a few select markets will be fully exposed to open and free trade policies. Government regulation and policy initiatives will be more frequent and complex. Markets and individual businesses will rise and fall with these events.

The challenge of getting new customers and keeping your current customers has become a virtual battlefield of conflicting forces. Every business day someone is focused on persuading your customers to switch to a competing product. There will be no respite from the accelerated pace of change or competition.

Now more than ever, the ability to compete successfully requires the careful selection of your adversaries and contests. Competing intelligently and efficiently will continue to grow in importance as the financial stakes increase. Understanding your competitors, as well as your purchasing audience, has reached a new level of importance. The requirement to evolve your products, business and competitive strategies constantly, before others displace your efforts, foretells a future belonging to the nimble and astute...

those who know how to win business from difficult competitors!

INDEX

E

G

I

K

L

M

N

O